# TWENTY-TWO MONTHS UNDER FIRE

# TWENTY-TWO MONTHS
# UNDER FIRE

BY HENRY PAGE CROFT

LONDON
JOHN MURRAY, ALBEMARLE STREET, W.
1917

# CONTENTS

## PART I

## THE TERRITORIALS

### CHAPTER I

### CHAPTER II

### CHAPTER III

### CHAPTER IV

### CHAPTER V

CONTENTS

# CONTENTS vii

CONTENTS

# PART II
# THE NEW ARMY

CONTENTS

# INTRODUCTION

WAR is one of those things the British people for nearly half a century have refused to contemplate, and the mere fact that the seas encircled the British Isles was sufficient to lull our people into a dreamland in which we pretended that a world war was impossible. War is an exacting thing: it demands great effort, it imperils wealth, it threatens luxury, it interferes with the sports and pleasures of the people—in a word, the idea of war was unpopular, and because it was unpopular, those who seek the favour of the British people and guide them avoided all mention of the ugly thing.

Preparation for war meant taxation, and how could any rising statesman, or still less any political party, advocate taxation when the fight for success in the political arena depended upon which section could promise most individual gain to the individual elector?

So it was that we drove war from the ambit of our thoughts, we of the British

race who have the greatest frontiers of the
world to defend, and from whom the world
has most to gain.

All parties ignored the overwhelming
evidence which hit us in the face from
Germany. No party would listen to Lord
Roberts and none was found to defend
that great man from the taunts and gibes
of second-rate political adventurers.

An annual expenditure on a national
army of five days' cost of this war would
have probably given us peace and most
certainly would have saved Belgium, and
deprived our enemies of that great start
which they gained whilst our patriotic people,
untaught, unorganised, unarmed, began to
learn the business of war.

The greatest Empire the world has ever
known at the striking of the decisive hour
of fate could only place four divisions in
the decisive theatre of war—that was the
prepared effort of 400,000,000 subjects of
our King.

This is not the hour to apportion the
blame, neither is it the moment to ask how
it was that the guardians of this great
heritage had failed, with such criminal
neglect, to organise the Empire and to
prepare for its defence. The time will come

when these questions will be asked with some persistence, then countless widows and orphans will demand an account of the stewardship which deceived and fooled the people, and finally plunged a nation into a war which was known to be imminent and for which no sort of preparation was made.

One fact stands out with a clearness that must be obvious, and that is, that the present political system of the British Empire has failed, and never again can issues of peace and war, or the defence of the Empire, be left in the hands of men whose sole obsession is political popularity, and who were so greatly occupied with party strife that they gambled with and risked the life of the greatest—yes, still the greatest nation on earth.

To the men of Oversea Dominions, whom I have lived with, fought alongside of, and learnt to admire on the field of battle, even more than in the days when I endeavoured humbly to serve the Imperial ideal at home, I would add this request: Do not judge our people by our political rulers, but rather join with the people of the old country to purify a system which is at fault, for whilst our politicians have failed, those also in the younger countries were little more successful in teaching the true path of patriotism—that freedom is of more worth than wealth.

We have learned together how to fight, and the blood of our dead is soaking the soil which they together have made immortal; let us now start out to design and build a palace on foundations of such depth and thickness that it shall stand for ever, but to secure this end, let us tolerate no half measures in the great memorial to our fallen. We have been up against hell for a common ideal, and whilst in the years to come each of our countries will work out as heretofore its own destiny, in those great matters which vitally concern us all and affect our common fate, let us come together in a complete, imperishable partnership.

This war has found the nations of the British standing together, fighting together, dying together, and is not the great lesson which it teaches and which the ages can never dim, first, that scattered as we are we can still claim similar qualities of steadfastness of purpose, courage against all odds, greatness in adversity, and humility in our hours of victory, and second that severally we could not have lasted the course, but together we shall win through ? The states of the Empire are essential one to the other, and henceforth we who have all to gain by the handclasp of fraternity will do well to enter a commonwealth in which we shall find our League of Peace, a commonwealth of all the British states.

In the hope and belief that out of the blinding dust and shattered wreckage of this war will come so great a good, I dedicate this little book of impressions to my comrades of the battlefield.

# PART I
# THE TERRITORIALS

# CHAPTER I

## THE GREAT ADVENTURE

WE were a subject of amusement to civilians and tolerated by regulars as an inferior article which probably meant well, but we continued in our spare hours to try and fit ourselves for the coming of " the Day." It occurred to us that the German nation was a practical one, and that if the day was not coming they would hardly squander the fruits of an amazing economic success in building a vast Navy and in increasing what was already the most complete military machine in the world. Further, if the Germans did not mean business why was the whole of their people ready to imbibe the doctrines of Bernhardi, and why did the countless writings of similar description find such a ready market amongst all classes of Germans ; why was the German Navy League encouraged to give lantern lectures to every school in Germany ; why was the final slide for the German youth always a picture of the sinking of the British fleet by that of Germany ?

The evidence was too strong, and so in the regiment to which I had the honour to belong we believed in the German peril, and in spite of laughter and taunts we decided to fit ourselves for the day. Three years before war was declared the 1st Battalion of the Hertfordshire Regiment was reported on as "fit for active service," and so we could afford to smile at those who asked us why we wasted our precious holidays in training—had not the regular soldiers themselves declared us worthy to fight with them when war came ?

.     .     .     .     .

The annual camp was taking place at Ashridge Park, Berkhampstead, and our training proceeded whilst some of us wondered about Europe.

The "Terriers" were playing at soldiers, and suddenly the Austrian ultimatum was sent and we knew our play was not in vain. We quickened our efforts; war burst on our country; our camp was broken up; and we realised we were to pay the proud penalty of patriotism.

.     .     .     .     .

We were business men, tradesmen, work-

ing men, each concerned in the profession
or job which we had made our life's affair,
and when the call came we had to break
with our life's work—no time for us to
settle our business, no time to find sub-
stitutes, our house was left in disorder,
and we marched towards the east coast.
Some day, when England has time to think,
she will thank her Territorials, who had to
make far the biggest sacrifice, and she
will realise that without the " peace time
patriot " the " regular Army " could not
have left her shores, and she will remember
that whilst the new armies were learning
to form fours without rifles or uniform,
which little details our thoughtful Govern-
ment had forgotten to provide, the Territorial units which had made good were
already proceeding to Belgium to fill the
shattered gaps of the immortal British Army.

.    .    .    .    .

We counted it a misfortune that we were
part of the East Anglian Division, because
it seemed that our very name would keep
us hugging the vulnerable shores of England,
perhaps till the end of all things, so we
settled down with no little restlessness to
training in the eastern counties ; but we
had forgotten the great general who had

declared us fit for war, and on November 2nd, 1914, we got our orders for the front. The Hertfordshire Regiment became very unpopular with the rest of the division, for had we not been chosen to go to the centre of the world whilst all the other battalions stayed behind?

.    .    .    .    .

It was in the early hours of the morning, the sleepy Suffolk town was still more sleepy than usual as we said good-bye to our women, and were assured by them that of course we were only going to defend the lines of communication. Oh yes, we said, of course it means the lines of communication! Quietly in the early morning we fell in by companies and then marched for the station with mighty song, whilst nightcaps and other unusual garments appeared in the windows as we sang our way to the train.

.    .    .    .    .

Our comrades of the brigade sent a band to play the train off—to play the "lucky devils" away to the place where men meet men. "See you soon," said the men of the rest of the brigade! Little we thought that within a year so many of the rest of

the brigade would perish in Gallipoli, when
they too became "lucky devils."

So long, see you soon!

. . . . .

Southampton; packed like flies in a ship
equipped for artillery—a hard bed this,
and how we used to groan at a straw bed
in a splendid farm barn! Havre—yes, there
it is, full of transports. Hospital ships,
ugh! A weary wait as the transport is
disembarked. A regiment of yeomanry
marches past—" good old Territorials!"—and
now we are off on French soil for the camp.

Crowds of French civilians line the streets
of Havre, fluttering handkerchiefs, friendly
smiles, "êtes vous les Gardes?"—Yes, the
Herts Guards—great laughter and much
singing, pretty faces in the upper windows.
We begin to talk French—such French!
and we have a comfortable feeling that now
we have arrived France is saved.

. . . . .

The rest camp—oh yes, we shall probably
be here for a fortnight; but what a camp!
depressing, "not 'arf"; let's be getting on!
Short route march next day; we shall probably do this every day, nobody knows how
long.

Splendid dinner in a restaurant this second

night in France.  But who is this disturbing
the coffee ?  An orderly, with orders to move
at 3 a.m. : five hours to get back to the
battalion, sleep and strike camp.  The authorities seem to be in a great hurry.

.    .    .    .    .

A weird march in the early morning pitch
dark, arrival at the station ; wait here for
orders, so the whole battalion lies down
on the cobbles.  Dawn comes, and parties
of men of many British regiments steal by
from the station.  Tired men, weary men,
ragged men, men who have been " there,"
and who are recovering from slight ailments
and soon to return.

.    .    .    .    .

The train at last—all aboard for no one
knows where.  How long the journey is,
how slowly the train moves !  The second
morning early we arrive at St. Omer.
There is much speculation as to our duties.
Some say that we shall form the body-
guard of the Commander-in-Chief; some say
we shall stay here in reserve.

.    .    .    .    .

We march to our first French village to
get acclimatised—the hint is given us that
we shall be here some time, probably a
fortnight ; we also learn that the attacks on

the British line at Ypres have been terrific.
We do some field work and drill, and we
can hear the guns quite plainly.

The Commander-in-Chief was here this
morning. He only saw one company, but
he said nice things to be conveyed to all
of us. We come to the conclusion we are
splendid fellows!

We are to do an attack practice before
staff officers from St. Omer; all goes well,
the attack practice is carried out just
according to book. The staff officers express surprise—why should they express
surprise! Next day off to dig; probably
we shall dig every day for a fortnight.
Yes, that is what we are here for. We
site the trench with field of fire in places
fifty yards. Oh yes, " capital field of fire,"
says the expert; but say we, this isn't the
book. Never mind, you've got fifty yards.
Yes, we must hit 'em at fifty yards.

.        .        .        .        .

Dig away, come on, you must get down;
don't mind how tired you get, show these
regulars what we can do! We are really
getting quite tired—what's this? Orders
to move at once to join the 4th Guards
Brigade at Ypres—quite right too; Herts
Guards to the Guards Brigade; but what

fools we were to dig so hard, and there is a six-mile march back to billets.

.    .    .    .    .

Buses; rows of buses—Marble Arch, Putney—half an hour to pack up—got to start at once. Load up outside and inside. Quite amusing at first this journey, but as the hours slipped by more and more fatiguing.

The road is full of interest. British and French cavalry, gunners and infantry in small parties, a stream of Red Cross cars— these latter seemed never to end—and then the rain descended and half the battalion for hours had to endure a soaking in the dark as the buses skidded this side and that; and then still more Red Cross cars, and one began to realise that we were nearing the edge of things.

.    .    .    .    .

All my life the persistent theory had held my mind that if ever I went into action I should run away the instant I came under fire, and now this fateful experience seemed to be imminent. The hours in that bus were spent in thought, with little consolation; and the weariness of the journey, coupled with the discomfort of those outside in the wet, tended to expel even excitement, and so the recurring question, " How

shall I behave under fire?" I expect many
have asked themselves this same question,
perhaps with equally unsatisfactory results.

I turned to history, and wondered how
my forbears felt on similar occasions, and
I remembered one, a bishop, who whilst
the soldiers of Cromwell tried to stop him
preaching in Hereford Cathedral, calmly
finished his sermon—which was on sacrilege—
whilst the soldiers kept their muskets aimed
at his head. I now came to the conclusion
if I had been in the pulpit, I should on
the appearance of the soldiers have speedily
pronounced the blessing and let the congre-
gation disperse.

.      .      .      .      .

At last, about midnight, we pulled up in
Vlamertinghe and "debussed," if that is
the right expression, into a dreary street,
whilst the rain came down in torrents and
rations were served out—a tiresome business
at any time, especially so when the food
was all packed on the last bus (which did
not arrive for an hour after the head of
the column), and had to be issued in pitch
dark whilst all ranks were soaked through.

One had time to look around, and here
again, whilst we waited, a very large number
of French Red Cross wagons kept passing,

whilst the sky was bright with the flash of the guns and we had our first education in the music of artillery.

.    .    .    .    .

After waiting some time, a staff officer came up and uttered the cheery words, " You will go to a farm to-night," and we all thought of nice barns, straw, and coffee, etc. Things were very lively, he told us; " they have made a big effort to smash us, and to-day their attack has been on a very big scale, but we have held them. . . . I think we will take the long road ; they have been shelling both heavily to-day, but the long road least." Oh yes, " How nice ! " we said.

# CHAPTER II

NEAR midnight we were ready to march, and conducted by our guide we set off on the road to Ypres. The rain ceased, and we entered the ancient city under a bright moon. The stricken town was very silent, although in the distance we could hear the incessant artillery duel. Sometimes we had to go slow, owing to the ruins of a house being scattered over the road; here we saw houses still burning after the day's bombardment, then a body huddled in a corner, and we knew that this was war.

On we marched until suddenly the grand old building of the Cloth Hall loomed up before us in all its beauty, that edifice which within a week was to fall, shattered by the unsparing guns of the enemy; and so on we went when suddenly, what was that? Swish—crash! a blinding flash all round the head of the battalion, and before

13

we had recovered from our surprise, again swish-crash, this time all in one; and as tiles and bricks fell round us I found myself knocked on my knees with a dull thud on my back. For a moment the head of my company was scattered over the road, but only for a moment. " Any one hit ? " Nothing serious, only half a dozen bruises, " lead on." Now shrapnel was freely bursting over the centre and rear of the battalion, and we marched on through the zone, and we in front began wondering how many casualties behind. So this is war. When will my turn come ? Will it be to-night, to-morrow, or next week ? Somehow I hoped it might be a week !

On we marched, ever nearer the inferno, and now the roll of rifle fire was incessant, and the high ground of Zonnebeke and Zillebeke was continually lit up by gun-flash and bursting shrapnel. The men were very tired, for, remember, we had been early afoot digging at St. Omer that day, and had marched twelve miles before we ever took our trip on the bus to this happy land.

.     .     .     .     .

Halt ! A château, the divisional head-quarters of Sir Charles Munro. Fresh guides, and on again to our cosy farm ! Arrived

at last; three companies will go into the
rest trenches, and one in the farm. Rest
trenches indeed, as we stumbled through
the dark and sorted ourselves out in a
maze of glorified ditches—oh the lucky
beggars in the farm!

Mount sentries. Where are we, where are
the enemy, where is our firing line? God
only knows! and so to sleep on the sodden
mud, which was oozing from hours of rain.

. . . . .

Early awake, those who had slept through
the artillery row, and shivering with cold,
we started to munch biscuits, and a few
more adventurous spirits managed to kindle
little fires to cook a hot drink, and so our
first morning in Armageddon hailed us—
the morning of November 12th, 1914.

# CHAPTER III

## EXCITEMENT

WE reasoned amongst ourselves that of course they will rest us to-day after our exacting experiences of yesterday, but " they " are unreasonable people evidently, because we had hardly begun to accustom ourselves to the enjoyment of life in a muddy field when suddenly a staff officer galloped up and in a very unemotional voice, speaking very slowly, told us that the French had been driven in on our left and that we were to go up behind them and dig a new line.

We decided to cultivate unemotional ways, and in unemotional voices ordered the fall in. By now our field guns on the left were barking like so many packs of angry dogs, and as my company was ready first I was again ordered to lead off; it is a bad habit that one, of being ready first.

We marched off, without waiting for the

battalion to close up, along a light railway line for about a mile and a half, and learnt how inconsiderate the British field gunner can be; for firing from about fifty yards on the other side of the railway they appeared to be trying to see how nearly they could miss taking our caps off, doubtless because they resented the fact that we had not already doffed to the immortal British gunner. And here were some of them actually cooking meat as we were advancing to the storming of Badajoz, or was it Waterloo itself?—nasty fellows, how I hate the smell of cooked meat! and my breakfast had been a biscuit and an inch of chocolate.

Things sounded brisk, and we reached a certain spot where his unemotional highness told our colonel he wished us to dig in. My colonel—Lord Hampden—without any discussion tells me to take my company on half a mile and cover the digging operations of the battalion, and I drew myself up awaiting his valedictory message, and fully expecting him to say, " Good luck! I know I can rely on you to hold out to the last whilst the battalion digs in; have you any messages for home ? " But this was the only time my colonel disappointed me, and no great and inspiring words did he utter.

3

C Company therefore pursued its way; and as we approached the brow of a hill I found a good hedgerow, which would at any rate form cover from view, and C Company began to dig in and die.

Now the view looking through this said hedge was interesting; there was a lot doing in the way of shell fire in front, and shells were whistling over our heads from the wrong direction, whilst small parties of Frenchmen could be seen trickling back, which confirmed me in my view that we were going to have some shooting. I told the men to dig like beavers, and this they did, in spite of the fact that they had only entrenching tools. I was well armed with a magnificent sword, and I suddenly realised that if these jolly shrapnel chaps began spraying my hedge there was no cover for me, whilst all my lads were already down some inches. So I began to dig in with my sword, and remembered—oh ghastly memory!—that hedge-lines should be avoided, as they are a good target for artillery. Still, if we went in front we should be spotted, and if we dug in in rear we should see nothing, so I stuck to my hedge-line and continued to excavate in this odd manner.

After an hour or so fresh batteries of

French artillery galloped up in rear and
began to open fire, and I saw a group of
the greatest ruffians life had yet presented
to me coming through our lines.  They
were pale, hairy-faced men in kilts ; and as
they came to me I realised they were British
Highlanders.  And then I heard their story.
They had been in a bayonet charge in a
wood two days before, and had lost their
unit—this was the first sight I had of the
defenders of Ypres, and they were not
good to look upon ; only later did I realise
that looks are nothing, and that those
unshaven, weary men, were part of the
most perfect troops that ever took to fighting—the British Expeditionary Force.

By the afternoon my lads had dug down
well and we began to feel the comfort of
earth walls, and at three o clock we heard
that only a small section of the French
line had given and that a counter attack
had regained it.  So all was well, and later
we would march back to our home of the
previous night—no Waterloo to-day.

Now I discovered a little farmhouse close
by, and in it a dead goat, a sack, and a
small pile of bean straw.  I left the goat,
as he was rather an aged corpse, but I
gathered up a nice bundle of bean straw

and the sack; and when we marched back
I may have looked odd, but that night I
lay on bean straw and both my legs went
into the sack with bean straw round my
feet. After this invention I never parted
with my sack, and later, in those trying
frosty nights, every man in my company
had two sand-bags in which he put his feet
at night.

During the afternoon we were introduced
to Herr Jack Johnson, but we took a dislike
to him at first sight. He comes over with
a respectable easy-going sound; there is a
pause, and then suddenly, with fateful wump,
up tears a great volume of smoke with
earth and anything else upon which the
gentleman alights; and if you go and look
where he pitched you find an excavation
of circular discription large enough to bury
a motor-bus in.

Now Jack Johnson is a sociable fellow,
and so he came over with three pals searching for human food. At first I thought it
was a sort of ducks-and-drakes game, as
four great explosions followed down a road;
but I then learnt that it was a battery of
four searching. He is not a tidy chap at
all, and throws his excavation sometimes
about a quarter of a mile, so that when

you are really enjoying him at a distance
you may suddenly be felled by a clod of
earth or, worse still, a piece of metal, when
really you are not part of the show.  This is
unfair, but I believe not really intended.
I am told the best place to be when a Jack
Johnson is around is about twenty yards
from the edge of his future crater, as then,
unless you are concussed, you are not hurt,
the effect of his disturbance being chiefly
upwards and outwards after his original
excavation is completed.  But as a rule,
people do not attempt to prove this theory.

I often wondered why we heard so much
of " coal boxes " in the beginning of the
war, but I soon discovered that there was
a certain shell not often used, which as it
took its airy flight made a noise just as if
you were throwing coal out of a scuttle
on to the fire.  I do not know whether this
meant a defective shell or whether it was
abandoned by the Huns, but I never heard
it after I left Ypres.

Well, by now we had seen lots of things,
and personally I had decided that with
luck they might be dodged for a fortnight.

# CHAPTER IV

## ZONNEBEKE

DURING these days the great effort of the Germans to pierce the British line at Ypres was reaching its end, but no one knew when fresh hordes of the Hun would not hurl themselves against our line, and now we were visited by our Divisional General, Sir Charles Munro, who came to our farmhouse.

The general is a typical Great-Briton, with bright eyes, a rugged countenance, middle height, with big shoulders and a cheery way which endears him to all he meets. "Well," he said, "I'm glad to see you; how glad perhaps you can realise when I tell you yesterday my reserves for the division were one platoon!"

Just what this means I doubt if England will ever realise, but I will try inadequately to explain. The 2nd Division, named by our friends the enemy the "Iron Division," after playing a marvellous part in the great

22

retreat, at Landrecies and again on the Aisne, exhausted in all but spirit and wasted to a fraction of its former self in numbers, was then hurried in the great strategic rearrangement to hold the line at Ypres. Here, shelled as no troops had ever been, day after day for weeks, the division bore the brunt of the tremendous efforts of the flower of the Kaiser's army to pierce our line. No story will ever rival that of this unequal contest when, pounded all day and night by an overwhelming mass of metal of hideous sounding high explosives to which we had no reply, these mighty soldiers of England—one man to five yards —stood steady always, and rolled back day after day the massed attacks of an unceasing stream of magnificently trained opponents.

Sometimes here or there a few yards of trench might give, because all the defenders were slain ; and then on their way up to their parts of the line a company or two would be gathered together and clear the penetrators out with the bayonet, but never, never once did the line bend before the human avalanche.

These were the days when the enemy advanced singing " Rhineland ! " when dense columns would march direct against our line and, as the leading fours rolled over, others marching straight over the bodies of their fellows pressed on, themselves to be withered by the most accurate and highly disciplined fire that a scanty line of defenders had ever exercised.

One day, so I was told, as the Prussian Guards advanced in their columns against our line, the leading fours were seen to be locked arm in arm, and some of the leaders, so rumour had it, marched blindfold, so that they might not fear to press on. But heroic as their attacks were, the Prussian Guards had met their match, for the British Guards—Cavan's 4th Guards Brigade—were there in front of them, and met them with a deadly fire, like some great dam against which a flood is checked, and they faded away like mist before a gale.

The true odds of the great defence of Ypres will probably never be told, but probably from start to finish some half a million of the absolute pick of the Germans made the most terrific punch in history, chiefly against three British divisions of a strength of about 30,000 men. When— British people—you sometimes wonder whether all is well with the nation, turn your thoughts to this grand epic, and your

backs will straighten, your chins will elevate
a little, and perhaps you will have to bottle
a tear of pride when you remember these
glorious figures, the saviours of Calais, who
rest there, covered lightly by the soil of
Ypres.

.      .      .      .      .

This, then, was the division in which we
found ourselves—the 2nd Division—although
we had not yet gained contact with our
Brigade, the 4th Guards, which was not
surprising, because in these fierce days the
Guards had themselves been separated in
the juggling of the line as each fresh phase
of the attack took place; and as for the
Brigadier, Lord Cavan, I believe I am right
in saying that he was shelled out of four
different head-quarters in two days, and
so he had no time to pay courtesy visits.

Boche now made a big effort against the
Zonnebeke position, and a short part of
the line was driven in.

It was on this famous occasion, I believe,
that a certain colonel of gunners, finding
that the Prussian Guard had penetrated
a small section of the front, lined up his
orderly-room staff, servants, cooks, and
any one he could collect in the road, and
opened fire on the enemy, thus making

Boche believe that he had run up against a second line. Anyhow, time was given for a counter attack to be collected, and the 52nd (Oxford and Bucks), who had only just been taken out of the line, were recalled. The Irish Guards attacking on the right through a wood with the bayonet, a company of the H.L.I. hurriedly rushed up and the 52nd on the left, the gap was filled and the position restored. When I mention that in this counter attack a field company of R.E. joined in the counter attack to save the situation, the position will be appreciated.

.        .        .        .        .

It was to this interesting scene, then, that we were on November 14th ordered to go and relieve the much tired 52nd, and some of our officers were sent on to reconnoitre the position.

We arrived at brigade head-quarters, my impressions of which were a little cottage with several holes in the wall, considerable noise from artillery all round, liquid freezing mud everywhere; and in this scene of noisy desolation two privates of the King's (Liverpool Regiment) splashing through the mire after an old hen which the guard of our brigade head-quarters apparently considered a disreputable old lady, whom it was their

duty to arrest. Whilst our C.O. was pow-
wowing with the colonel of the 52nd we
had to wait about in the bitter cold, but
on being welcomed into the guard room
by the sergeant of the guard we were presented with cups of steaming chicken broth,
and I found my sympathies, which had
previously been with the hen, were now
wholly on the side of the guard.

We walked through a wood to see the
left of our line, where we joined the King's,
and walked down a ride on which our left
rested, where we paused, and I curiously
looked round the corner of the wood, when
I was yelled at by our colonel friend, who
explained that, if I showed myself there,
not only would I die from an enemy bullet,
but, far more important, the whole party
might get shelled! And so it is that we get
less curious as we get older. He also
explained that half the battalion would
rest in this wood whilst the other half was
in the trenches, that frequently the wood
was shelled and that it was therefore advis-
able to keep the men in the holes provided
for them (dugouts were a later invention,
and no one had up to now had time to dig
to any depth).

At dusk the battalion arrived, and as

soon as it was dark I proceeded with my
company overground to my allotted trench,
where I relieved a company of the 52nd.
Whilst this relief was going on, bullets
were spitting and cracking round us all the
time, and I thought that many would be
hit; but I was green, and as a matter of fact
we suffered no casualties.

The so-called trench was for the most
part a series of holes, and not at all a nice
place for officers, as instead of walking
along a trench to see if the sentries were
awake, I had to walk continually along the
top. To-morrow night I vowed that we
would scrape some sort of a trench in spite
of the zipping of the bullets. The men of
the 52nd were amazed at the impudence
of a Territorial battalion coming up to
hold their line—the line of the bloody
fight of two days previous, but they were
mighty glad to see us for all that, and
Territorials went up a point or two in their
estimation. That night I could not sleep ;
excitement kept me awake, for the sudden
bursts of rifle fire to our right and left
showed that liveliness was still in these
parts; but I dozed off for a few minutes as
I stood in my hole, and then I felt something
soft and wet pressed against my face. I

woke with a start, to hear a strange yet not unfamiliar noise, to discover that an old sow and her litter of pigs had come to pay her call on the Hertfordshire Regiment. I believe that some pork was enjoyed the next evening, but as the nearest inhabitants were miles away, I think that the loot was, under the circumstances, not very wicked.

After this experience I decided to venture into a farmhouse immediately in rear, and told a sentry to come to me half an hour before dawn.

I struggled through a very muddy yard and was glad to get under a roof, and laying myself down slept in great comfort for two hours. The sentry woke me up, as I thought, rather violently and with a very scared look on his face, and only then, by the light of a match, did I discover that within a yard of me lay the corpse of a Prussian Guardsman. I stole back to my company, feeling that exploration was not always pleasant, and nearly tripped over several bodies in the yard, where Connaught Rangers and Prussians had been killing each other four days before.

I was glad to get back to my hole, sow or no sow, and there gave the order to stand to. As dawn came—our first in the trenches—an extraordinary sight unfolded itself, for over the field in front of us were scores of great grey bodies, of the men of the Kaiser's Guard, some lying facing us who had fallen in the attack, others facing away who had been killed when our counter attack took place. Up to now we had most of us felt a good deal of the sport of war, but here we were up against the reality, for all around was death, and we graduated into the ranks of campaigners.

My company was only kept forty-eight hours in these trenches, when we went to the aforementioned wood and were relieved by another company of our battalion. Arriving in the wood late at night we were shown the dugouts in which we were to rest ourselves, but unfortunately we discovered that these residences were not very spacious. My first decision, therefore, was to lie outside under the trees; but as bullets began cracking against the trees all round us, I soon came to the conclusion that crushed sleeping quarters were better than the simple life above ground.

The effect of bullets penetrating a wood is very strange until you get accustomed to them, and I remember this night I was under the impression for quite a consider-

able time that there were German snipers
actually in the wood, firing at us with rifles
which made less noise than usual. This
was because the crack of the bullet sounded
like the crack of a rifle, especially when they
hit a tree in one's immediate neighbourhood. Thus at one moment I was almost
convinced that a German was firing at me
from about thirty yards' distance, and accordingly kept my revolver out and my head
down. This is one of the illusions which
add to the excitement of the moment, but
which is soon exposed. However, that night
I slept in a hole with both of my subalterns
sleeping on top of me, a most uncomfortable
proceeding, but I reasoned it out that my
fifteen stone odd, had the position been
reversed, would have resulted in no subalterns for C Company the next morning.

    .    .    .    .    .

The next day, as we were all profoundly
convinced that there were snipers in the
wood, the two companies quartered there
decided to have a drive and to try and bag
a German, so they extended through the
wood and, in the best covert shooting discipline, drove the wood, but no live Germans
were discovered, although we had the satis-
faction of learning afterwards that our drive

had succeeded to the extent of one German, who fled straight into the lines of the King's Liverpool and was duly annexed. The only live German whom we bagged through this tour was an officer of the Prussian Guard, who was found wounded in a hole. He had remained alive since the Prussian Guard attack, and was extremely grateful for the care we bestowed upon him and afterwards, I believe, recovered.

.        .        .

We now heard, with great joy, that the French were coming up to relieve us ; and if we were gladdened by such tidings, just imagine what the feelings must have been of the remainder of the division, who had been in the line nearly a month without relief, and who had had such hard fighting previously.

It was my good fortune to see a good deal of the British regular battalions who were holding the line at this time, and from every point of view the odds against them were such that one wondered how on earth the positions had been held for so long. There was only one thing which surprised one more, and that was the spirit of the troops who had seen such a very large proportion of their comrades wiped out, and into whose heads the idea never seems to have entered that the line could possibly be broken by the enemy. This, notwithstanding the fact that the Germans were ten to one, that their artillery outnumbered us at every point, and their heavy guns were pounding our positions continually without any reply of the same description from us!

The regular army knew that it would be months before the new army could be formed, and yet this indomitable little host were so sure of themselves that I firmly believe that none of them would have been surprised if they had been ordered to make a general attack upon the enemy—"some spirit," as the Americans would say.

.    .    .    .    .

4

# CHAPTER V

## RELIEVED BY THE FRENCH

THE news that the French were coming to relieve the British troops at Ypres spread very quickly through all ranks, and in spite of the bitter cold and wet, every one became very cheerful. Such a big relief could not of course take place all at once, and it was decided to relieve the left of the line where we were first, and I was sent off with two other officers on the morning of the 16th to reconnoitre the route where the French were coming, so as to be able to guide them up to our trenches during the night. We set off across country, and had not gone more than a quarter of a mile before we suddenly found shrapnel falling round us, whereupon we precipitated ourselves upon the earth for a second, jumped up again, when another shrapnel burst right amongst us, one bullet of which penetrated through all the clothes of one of our company

Commanders without hurting him. We came to the conclusion that the German artillery must be able to see us and were sniping at us with field guns, and accordingly we moved on at a most undignified pace over that piece of country. As a matter of fact, the shelling was chance searching by the Germans and we could not really be seen, but we were still novices at the game. We were directed to go to certain head-quarters a mile from our wood, where we would be told where and when to expect the French. The said head-quarters were a tiny cottage occupied by the head-quarters staff of two historic British battalions. As we entered the little door the scene presented to us will not easily be forgotten.

Under the dim light of one candle some eight officers were gathered round a table, and it is hard to imagine signs of greater physical fatigue than were evidenced on their faces; but they were all typical officers of the old regular army : that type which never shows surprise and which considers every question with dignity and without emotion.

I have no hesitation in saying that the greatest strength of the British officer lies in the fact that he is trained, from his earliest

days in the profession, not to get excited
and to take things quietly, and I believe
that this is one of the principal reasons
why regular officers have such a great
ascendancy over their men, for the appearance of silent strength under any circumstances must give confidence in war.

Walking into this cottage in our com-
paratively smart khaki with polished buttons,
and finding ourselves amongst these men
with the distant look in their eyes which
comes from continual strain, we felt we
had entered a new world. No one an-
nounced they were glad to see us or asked
us any curious questions; no one patronised
us as Territorials; we were simply treated
as if we were members of the mess who
came in every day to report for orders.
Our friends soon served us with steaming cups of cocoa, whilst we sat in that little
room crushed up into a small space—how
often in future were we to be crushed into
small spaces! As we sat we discussed the
question of the relief by the French, and
we were strongly recommended to reconnoitre a cross-country route in order to
save the French two miles of road that
was almost impossible owing to the mud,
and having been directed, off we went to

the point where we were to meet the French later in the day, and thence we reconnoitred the route we had to go.

Sights in that wood will not easily be forgotten, for it was here where the Germans temporarily gained a footing in our line and had been driven out by a bayonet attack. By marking trees we came to the conclusion that we would be reasonably certain to find our way in the night. In order to make this short cut, however, part of the route was just behind some trenches held by the Northamptonshire Regiment. We were somewhat dismayed to see that we should have to take the whole battalion of Frenchmen across a field where they would not be 300 yards from the enemy, so we made up our minds that somehow we must convey this fact to our French friends when we took them up.

There was a stable and cottage by the side of the road where we had to wait for the French, but the stable was by no means sweet, so we lay down in the road; but as it became dark we discovered that the road was a most unhealthy place, since bullets came ripping our way continually, and occasionally a Maxim gun swept straight along it, so we tucked ourselves under a wall

in as sheltered a place as we could be whilst
the bullets spluttered against the cottage.
Whilst we were waiting here we saw stretcher
parties going by with various British
wounded—that procession which had gone
by daily for nearly a month and which,
after to-night, would be no longer a British
procession.

At last a messenger came to tell us that
the French were approaching, and we went
out to meet them. The battalion lay
down on the side of the road whilst the
French commandant, with his officers, came
into the stable to make his dispositions for
the relief. A candle was produced, and
there Mons. le Commandant and his
officers, none of whom knew a word of
English, wrestled with us, who knew hardly
a word of French, over the intricacies of
the relief operation which was about to
take place. After about three-quarters of
an hour, by the use of maps and pigeon
language, the whole thing was cleared
up, and we struck up a great friendship
with our French comrades, who shook us
repeatedly by the hand, but for some reason
or other did not offer to kiss us. After
finally imploring them with many gesticula-
tions to impose silence upon their men and

to *non fumer,* which we imagined was an injunction not to smoke, we set off on our night's march.

The Frenchmen behaved very well in going by the difficult spot, and they might have been a thousand mice. But when we got into the wood the whole battalion got very animated, and I comforted myself by reflecting that such was the noise that the enemy would be under the impression that a large number of jays had returned to those parts. Whenever we passed what was once a German soldier, the Frenchmen, in single file, could be heard uttering what, I am sure, were terrible oaths, right back to the end of the battalion; equally if we passed a dead Englishman, they would give expression to their feelings of compassion.

Having eventually reached the edge of the wood, we were about 100 yards from the right of my battalion; but as we were coming from the right front, where the line bent forward and there was a small gap, I was rather anxious that the Herts Regiment should not test its marksmanship upon us, so I crawled forward to where I knew there was an isolated post, suddenly to hear a very fierce whisper and to observe a bayonet flashing under the moon, challenging me. However, having assured the sentry that we were decent folk, up to no mischief, I went back and brought the French along. The relief was carried out without any difficulty, each Frenchman tumbling into his hole as our men climbed out. The French commandant, instead of sleeping in a dugout, insisted that he would go and sleep in my farmhouse of three nights before. I used all my persuasiveness, and invented wonderful words to explain to him the horrors of that *non-bon* place; but apparently the French officer, even if a house is known to be shelled at all times or possesses other residential drawbacks, prefers to sleep therein to anywhere else.

By this time it was late at night, and our battalion began to march back to the rest trenches which we had previously occupied at Kilometre 3 on the Ypres–Menin Road. The road was in an indescribable state, slimy chalk mud about half a foot deep, and there were a nasty number of bullets flying about.

When we reached Weston Hoek we were delayed for a long time, as various British regiments marched back on relief. The road was very congested and movement

slow, and as Boche began shelling we were
not very delighted at our enforced wait
whilst the endless stream passed us on the
main road. Meanwhile, we heard that our
medical cart had got bogged and was temporarily abandoned. We did, however, at
last arrive back at Kilometre 3, and there,
to my joy, I heard that my company was
to have the privilege of going to the farm,
and it was not long before C Company was
fast asleep, and noticeably its commander,
who had been on the go for over eleven
consecutive hours after four nights of little
sleep.

# CHAPTER VI

## REAL SHELLING

BLESSED are those who are not luxurious, for they shall have a peaceful time!

As I explained, my company now had the luxury of the farm building, and we had the laugh of the rest of the battalion, which lay down to rest in the freezing mud. We had a comfortable night, my bed being that on which many a weary cow had laid herself to rest. We rose late for our ablutions, feeling very peaceful in mind, when suddenly we heard a whistling through the air, followed by a most terrific explosion which was evidently somewhere inside the farm. The whole of the company was immediately got out of the building and ordered to double to the trenches; but before they had all got clear from the farm, another shell of similar gigantic proportions exploded, killing one lad and knocking over half a dozen others. I was still in the cows' stall, hastily donning my puttees, when a third shell pitched into the yard itself, and the air was a mass of debris all around. I called out to the three officers' servants who were left in the stables to get clear of the building at once and ran to the door, where I discovered a terrified horse belonging to one of our mounted officers, tied up to the wall; and it was fortunate for me that it was so, as I jumped on his back and galloped, and had only just cleared the farmyard when a fourth shell pitched right on the stable which I had just left. All three of the officers' servants had been badly wounded, and we decided to keep away from these farm buildings in future.

There is no doubt that some German aeroplane had spotted this farm and had directed their 8-inch guns to fire upon it, and the shooting was indeed remarkable. The farmhouse itself was not touched, and the old Belgian farmer and his wife, with three young refugees, continued to live in this house and to farm their land regardless of the warning which they had received.

We now continued to live a very crowded existence in the rest trenches, whilst all the time the enemy kept throwing heavy stuff all around us.

The same afternoon we had an unexpected order to march to Zillebeke to relieve the 10th Hussars and the Royals, who were holding that part of the line.

# CHAPTER VII

## ZILLEBEKE

WE were feeling anything but fresh before we started on our march to Zillebeke—not that we had taken any exercise, but there is nothing more tiring than to sit still all day in poor shelters under heavy shelling, and especially is this true of new troops, who think that every shell is specially directed at them and who can hardly distinguish the noise of the burst of an enemy shell from that of their own guns. After a time the experienced soldier knows when a shell is high up or going to his flanks, and realises that not every missile that hurtles through the air has his own name and number inscribed thereon.

Soon after dusk we moved off along a slimy road, whilst the night got colder and colder. After dodging many shell holes, which we had difficulty in discerning owing to the liquid mud that filled them, we came to

Zillebeke village, or what remained of it.
A battered church still looked like a church,
houses dishevelled and war-broken still
stood tottering or with roof stripped bare ;
but ruin, stark ruin, seemed to stare at us
from every side. In many of these residences, where cover remained, little groups
of Frenchmen could be seen warming thumbs
round bright fires, and very picturesque
they looked in their baggy red trousers.
It was a mystery whence these Frenchmen
came or to what units they belonged, but
they seemed at any rate to be masters of
the art of making themselves at home, and
there were many little tricks we decided to
pick up from poilu before the weeks got
much older.

The traffic on the road was thick, and it
was some time after dark when we arrived
at Zillebeke Wood, where guides met us and
we continued our serpentine march to the
trenches.

The moon was now out and a hard frost
had set in as we wended our way through
the pine trees until we came to a comfortable
looking dugout, and the battalion was halted
whilst company commanders were ordered
up.

Very cosy within looked the dugout as

we entered to get our orders and were introduced to the squadron commanders of the
10th and the Royals whom we were to relieve.

We were soon moving on again on the
side of a little valley, down which rushed a
little stream, and our guides passed the word
" No smoking or talking ! " We came to
a ride which was swept at times, so we were
told, by a machine gun—my pace was
smarter across that ride—and so on until
we got to the line. Here again no trench,
just holes to hold two or three men, and
very quickly we slid in as the cavalrymen
climbed out. My Hussar guide told me
that we must be careful in the daytime, as
we were only sixty yards from the Hun.
" Really," I replied, in a voice which pretended to be barely interested as I stood
there three-score yards from Bocheland, whilst
bullets spat every few seconds through the
trees.

" Yes," said the phlegmatic one, " they
attacked this morning, but they can't rush
you ; there are so many trees down you can
hear them tumble ; besides, we have hung a
lot of jam tins on the wire."

" Will you go away, man, and let me get
into my hole ? " I whispered fiercely to
myself when at last he said, " Well, I must

be getting on. Poor —— had your dugout; he was killed this morning, shot through
the brain. It is absurd saying the Boches
cannot shoot."

" Quite absurd," I answered. " Good-
night ! "

The night became more frosty and we
could clearly hear Boche talking over there,
when suddenly, away on our right, rifles
began to crack, and then in the quiet of that
wood the cracking was taken up far to the
right and rolling right along in a crescendo
of sound till our men joined in; and again,
then on our left, and the roar of thousands
of rifles echoed through the night whilst
the split-splut thud of German ball ammunition played over our heads. We of course
imagined that the enemy were attacking.
After a while the firing died down again,
but twice during that night heavy firing
started, and again the crescendo of din
occurred, but this time it was the Huns;
and as we knew we were not attacking, we
merely stood to with our heads well down
and assured each other that the enemy had
" got the wind up."

In the early hours of the morning rations
were brought along and had to be distributed
in the open, whilst a lot of rifle firing went

on, and one began to realise how much lead can hurtle without finding its mark.

All ranks stood to early, and we awaited dawn in a hard frost and discovered the bolts of our rifles in many cases jammed by the freezing of the mud with which they had got covered in the night.

Just as the light of day was coming, and whilst we still could hardly discern any object clearly and trees looked like men, I heard a faint rustle in front of me; then suddenly, not thirty yards to my front, I saw a helmetted German, looking huge in the half light, stand straight up to step over a fallen tree; my hand was on my rifle, and I aimed; crack! and down he fell, just as sentries right and left of me also let drive, and the Hertfordshires accounted for their first Hun.

As I explained there was no trench, and all orders had to be passed along the line. I am sure this brave German had heard me passing orders, and had come to bag me in the half light, just as he had probably killed my predecessor in my hole the preceding day.

As daylight came, we began to see where we were, and very beautiful the wood looked with its coating of frost. Our position ran to my left fairly straight, but 100

5

yards to my right it bent back at right angles
across a ride, where we had a good view
through the wood for about 600 yards;
and here, during the day, our right company
got some good long-distance shooting, as
numerous Germans could be seen doubling
across the ride, especially in the evening,
when our lads claimed several hits, and we
got a machine gun into action down the
ride after dark.

Early the next morning German aeroplanes
were playing about in the sun over our
heads, and we wondered why they should
hover over us in this attentive manner.

We were not long left in doubt. For
several hours our right company was subjected to a shelling by German heavies,
such as would have tested any troops in the
world.

The shooting was remarkably accurate,
and soon casualties were reported in rapid
succession as Jack Johnsons fell all round
the holes in which our lads were trying to
take cover. Great masses of earth were
hurled into the air to crash down all along
the line; trees fell, and we, who were only
100 yards away, could only watch in silence
what looked like the decimation of our
comrades.

At midday I had a message thrown along from hole to hole in an empty jam tin to tell me that the company commander and his subaltern were both buried, and asking for orders.

Now they were at the apex of a triangle, and I thought that this shelling was probably the prelude to an attack, so I sent the first order which had ever made me hate myself, to the effect that they were to hang on, and that I would endeavour to replace their casualties. I sent back to another company commander to send up fifty men to reinforce our battered right; and whilst the inferno continued, the reinforcements came steadily up through the trees and lay down in the open wood just behind the trouble. Gradually they rushed, one at a time, through the danger zone, and so the gaps were filled. The attack which we had expected all day never came, and so our comrades went unavenged.

Of this company which had been so badly hammered, seven were killed by shell fire, two were never seen again and believed to be buried, seven were dug out alive, and some twelve others wounded.

We were much impressed with the necessity of a communication trench, which up

to then, owing to the scarcity of men, had
not been dug, since owing to our proximity
to the enemy we were cut off from head-
quarters, and stretcher bearers and orderlies
had little chance of getting through alive.

At seven o'clock that night the 2nd
Coldstream Guards relieved us, and right
glad we were, after a long and weary wait,
to stagger back, shaken, cold, and thirsty,
to our rest trenches on the Ypres–Menin
Road.

## CHAPTER VIII

REST, real rest, away from this clamour and din—how good that message was, for since we had been hurled into the vortex of this strange world, we had never been for a moment out of shell fire. We had seen men die, we had fed solely on bully beef and biscuits, and we had been either soaked to the skin or blue with cold—(I almost said funk).

All day long the French came trickling along the cobbled road from Ypres, fine fellows, laden with their heavy equipment, but not too heavy to prevent their carrying kettles and pots to add to their " Father Christmas " appearance.

The French tread very lightly, and they never march in step except through a town or on parade ; and often riding along in the dark I have found myself on top of a stealthy French battalion marching in

such different style to the steady tramp of
our British troops ; but they cover the
ground well, and the regular regiments of
the French Army give one a great feeling of
confidence as they move quietly about their
work without any fuss.

We had a good sample of French coolness
as we watched them this day, for whilst
they marched along the road a battery of
Jack Johnsons suddenly opened with salvos
along the road, and the French battalion
very soon scattered into artillery formation
of little groups of eight men in the fields
on either side of the road. There was no
confusion and no apparent alarm when
suddenly a shell burst right in front of a
little group ; three men fell dead, one
retired back wounded, and the other four
calmly put the dead in the crater made by
the shell, covered them up, placing a loose
piece of wood to mark the spot, and then
walked quietly on.

We had to wait till night for orders to
march, and I returned with two brother
officers to the farm from which I had fled
so precipitately a few days before, to see if
I could get a hot drink. The old Belgian
farmer and his plucky wife were still there,
clinging with the persistence of madness

to all they had lived for; and there, in one of the only rooms left standing, the little wrinkled old woman gave us huge bowls of steaming coffee.

Just as we were fully engrossed in this joyful task, suddenly crash, crash, crash, tiles flew and the house shook, but all the old lady said was " Bon, bon, shrapnel shrapnel," as she poured out more coffee. So this wonderful old lady could express pleasure that only shrapnel was crashing on her home and not high explosives which would finally destroy her! War indeed teaches us to see the proportion of things.

Their stable was flattened, half their house a mass of ruins, their barn now possessed one wall, and yet, indomitable soul, she could utter " Bon, bon, shrapnel! " I myself saw two men killed and five wounded in their very yard, but what happened to these two wonders I never heard; all I do know is that for those three bowls of coffee three golden sovereigns were gladly offered, and three British officers were sad to leave such brave hearts who had been caught in the clutches of war, but refused to flee the home of their ancestors.

.      .      .      .      .

We waited wearily for those orders which

never came, until at last at 10.45 p.m. the
message reached us. An orderly had tried
to find us earlier, but whichever way he
went he met a barrage of shell fire and had
to go some miles round.

.      .      .      .      .

Off at last, where we did not know, but
we knew it was for rest, and that is a wondrous
place.

To reach the main road we had to go in
the pitch dark by a side track, and here
a big shell had made an enormous excavation
right across the road, leaving only a goat
path for the infantry to creep by; but it
was my job to see the battalion past. Fortunately the transport had gone on early,
but there were still the pack-horses and
the medical cart to negotiate this obstacle.
By informing the pack-horses that they
were goats, we managed to get them all by
except one " unbeliever " which slithered
down to the bottom of the crater, and all
the King's horses and all the King's men could
not extract that pack-horse. The medical
cart was clearly checkmated, and so I left
the doctor to wait for dawn and bring the
pack-horse if he could; this with the help of
ropes he achieved early next morning.

.      .      .      .      .

What a march! By this time the head of the battalion must have nearly reached Ypres, and I was unable at first to catch the last company to ask leave to close up. The road was a sheet of ice and the pack-horses went down one after the other; it was pitch dark; two French battalions were passing us and a British cavalry regiment marching across the road, but at last I caught the rear of the column and passed up the word to halt.

.    .    .    .    .

Once more we marched through Ypres, but how changed from our last visit! This time whole rows of houses were in ruins, and the Cloth Hall was shattered—its ancient beauty gone for ever. The night was very cold, the wind cutting like a knife, and as we marched on down country roads men began to fall out, only to be cursed on again by my brutal self, for I knew that we had fifteen miles to go, and that a man who dropped now out, far away from houses and with no British troops behind, would suffer privation and worse, because to lie there that bitter night and sleep meant death.

At last, with few men out, we saw ahead great bonfires at Ouderdom, the half-way halt where we knew hot drinks awaited us.

Here the congestion was great, and it was another hour before we got to our field. Tommy, you are a strange fellow! No sooner did he lay down his kit, weary, cold, with frost-bitten feet, than he starts to sing, and all the world's a schoolyard and all the men are boys.

Tea is served out and a tot of rum, and for an hour we sing and try to get warm round the great fires and talk of rest. Now we are off again for Meteren in falling snow; the narrow roads are choked with traffic and we have to move in single file for miles. The men are "sticking it" well, but half the battalion is limping, and just as dawn breaks we begin to scale Mont Noir. Here on the steep ascent some scores of men drop out, for frostbite had found its victims. My horse does a side slip on the icy surface —crash we both go, but no bones broken and on again; now we are on the summit of the hill and the sun is up. The view is beautiful, for miles around appears a glorious landscape of snow-clad plains of Flanders, but the faces of our men are not beautiful; haggard and pale they struggle on, with pain in their every step.

Many men of many regiments are on the side of the road. They all have the war look!

that look which I, a stranger, had seen
when we came to Ypres, a look which I
had never seen before or since, and which
I hope never to see again.

So we came south from the first defence of
Ypres.

## CHAPTER IX

### GOD SAVE THE KING !

OUR stay at Meteren gave us a good chance of reorganisation, and we quickly pulled ourselves together. At first we found that quite 50 per cent. of the men were unable to march owing to frostbite; but luckily the trouble was only incipient, and after a week the whole battalion was on its feet again.

We now had opportunities of making the acquaintance of our brigade—the 4th (Guards)—and very welcome we were made, all ranks going out of their way to show that our intrusion was not resented. At first we were inclined to be astonished to see the Guards practising the slow march and other ceremonial movements in muddy fields, as I think we imagined we had left all that kind of thing behind; but it was not long before we followed suit and learnt the lesson which we never forgot, that steady drill after the trenches is the one way to keep discipline and " snap."

We received the following message from Brigadier-General the Earl of Cavan, commanding the 4th Guards Brigade :

The Brigadier would like to take this opportunity of welcoming the 1st Battalion Hertfordshire Regiment to the Brigade. From what he has already seen in the trenches and on the march, he is certain that the battalion will play a noble part in this great war. The battalion has already had hard work and lost some good comrades, but they left with their line intact, which is an achievement fit to rank in history with other great battles of the Army.

On November 23rd the brigade was inspected by the Commander-in-Chief, who addressed in turn the 2nd Grenadiers, 2nd Coldstream, 3rd Coldstream, 1st Irish, and Herts.

On this occasion we were almost ashamed of our strength, as we were far the strongest unit on parade, one of the Guards battalions parading only some eighty strong, commanded by a captain who brought them out of Ypres. Sir John French spoke with no little emotion when he thanked these

gallant remnants of the pick of our man-
hood for the wonderful part they had played;
but it was sad to remember how many of
these magnificent " six-footers " had gone
West, and that they had done their part
to save the line at such a terrible cost.

At the end of November the troops were
inspected by His Majesty the King, and
although the weather was cold and Flanders
looked its bleakest, it was an inspiring
sight to see the long straight roads lined
on either side by endless walls of khaki,
topped by the glint of thousands of bayonets.

The King, with the Prince of Wales,
General Officers, and Staff, walked down
the whole line, and each company hailed
him with tumultuous cheers as he reached
its head. I do not know whether one may
attribute thoughts to a King, but I believe
he was proud that day, as his soldiers were
proud of him. A few gracious words to
commanding officers, and he passed on to
fresh cheering ranks of other brigades.
" God save the King! "

. . . . .

This life of ease had to come to an end
soon, and on December 22nd we were ordered
to march to Bethune, where troublous times
were occurring.

# CHAPTER X

## FOR FIGHTING PASTURES NEW

IN the early hours of the morning the 4th Brigade assembled for the long march of nineteen miles to Bethune, near which town a very heavy attack had been made upon the Indian troops. To the Hertfordshires was given the honour of heading the brigade, and this put the battalion on their mettle, with the result that they reached their destination with only some ten men left on the road. For a considerable part of the way the Prince of Wales marched at the head of the Hertfordshire Regiment with our colonel. When we arrived at the outskirts of Bethune it was already dark, and we lay down on the banks of the canal waiting for orders as to billeting. It was a very quiet night, and a well-known songster in our battalion stood up by the side of the canal and began to sing with great success, the chorus being taken up by the

whole brigade, and the effect was most
striking. The British soldier is fond of
singing in the dark, but by day only a few
bold spirits take to song. At last our billeting parties sent guides, and the march proceeded to Bethune. The battalion marched
through the town as if they had come two
miles instead of nineteen, and the whole of
the inhabitants, hearing our marching songs,
turned out to welcome the brigade, and it
was quite exciting to all of us once more to
see the bright shop windows and evidences
of civilisation. We proceeded to the tobacco
factory, where we found a large number of
Indian troops already ensconced, and many
of them were seen in the yard, squatting
round little fires where they cooked marvellous Eastern dishes, greatly to the interest of all ranks of ours, many of whom
had never before seen an Indian soldier.

.      .      .      .      .

Very early the next morning the brigade
marched to Les Facons, where we had our
dinners during a slight snow storm in a
muddy field, and at dusk we moved up close
into support of the line, where we went
into some farm buildings, and on December
24th, officers were ordered forward to reconnoitre the line.

## CHAPTER XI

THE trenches we were about to take over were held by a battalion of Jats, and we were shown round the line by one of the four white officers left in this unit. The trenches were poor and wide, the Indians having had to dig in in a hurry along old ditches, which are always places to be avoided if time permits to entrench elsewhere. The Jat is a tall, handsome looking fellow, and has made quite a reputation on this front as a steady soldier, but it was pitiful to see how much they evidently felt the damp cold—indeed, it was a good thing they were to be relieved, because, as their officers told us, they had had a bad gruelling, and it is not good to hold a line when many of your comrades lie dead out in front.

In this particular sector there was a sap running out 150 yards in front of the line to within ten yards of a German sap, and here daily a British officer of this corps went up to snap shoot at the enemy with his revolver, just by way of showing how much kick the Jats had left in them.

These turbaned gentlemen, with their silky straight black hair, were very happy to think we were coming to see their habitation with a view to occupation, and the trenches became animated with chatter and much amiable advice to keep our heads down.

On the way back to the battalion, the enemy began to shell Dead Cow Farm and Chocolat Menier Corner. The former name needs no explanation; the latter was a cross-road in the Rue du Bois, where the advertisement of the famous firm stared you in the face on the wall of a corner house.

Now these high-explosive shells walked down the road with us, so to speak, as if to convey the intimation, "Nasty place this you have come to!"

A brother officer and I at the third " crump," which was in the yard of one of the houses about fifty yards off, began to run, but just at that moment a stream of Ghurkas came rushing out of their threatened billets, and so we had to pull up sharp and

walk very deliberately, pausing here and
there to admire the scenery ; however, the
next shell was some way off, so that our
dignity was not put to the supreme test,
and we strolled on whilst Johnnie Ghurka
returned to his house.

. . . . .

The line was relieved at night, and our tall
friends, with a goodly display of beautiful
white teeth, silently faded away as we made
ourselves at home in their trenches and
wondered whether the North Pole was really
cold.

There was a big gap away on our left,
but as we had no maps except for our
immediate trenches, we did not know that
a thousand yards to our left the line bent forward almost at right angles, and that we were
on the circumference of a semicircle.

An hour or two after we were settled
down that night a fairly heavy rifle fire
opened on us from our left, and as I was
in charge of the battalion in the line, I
ordered rapid fire in order that these dogs
of Huns might be silenced. We plumped
lead into the void, and they fired back with
some spirit, and so for half an hour the fire
fight went on until I ordered the cease fire.

Only next morning did I discover that

this fiercely contested battle had been joined, not with the detested Germans, but with His Britannic Majesty's most loyal and gallant Highland Light Infantry, and that the total casualties were, Herts Regiment, *nil.*, H.L.I. *nil.* I had to explain to the officers of our company that I thought they should correct their fire three-quarters right next night, as I feared they did not quite realise where their front was !

Little did I think during the year of 1902, when I was attached for several weeks to the H.L.I. as their guest, that 1914 would find me in a foreign land, ordering rapid fire on their devoted heads ; and I really had no grudge, for their hospitality was always lavish ; but they " hit me first," as the little boy always explains on these occasions.

# CHAPTER XII

## CHRISTMAS-TIDE

OUR first Christmas in the trenches was celebrated at dawn with rapid fire, and the festival was lively. Early in the day I got news that a lad who lived in my native town in Hertfordshire had been killed by a bullet whilst on sentry in the sap, and then it was that a sergeant in his company anxiously asked and received leave to go up and take his place.

The sergeant, who was a good shot, avenged the boy by killing the German sniper; but shortly afterwards a bullet through the brain sent him to join his young comrade. After this we began to study the art of sniping, and the tactics of the hunter were added to the science of shooting.

It was a cold, sharp day, and we received various gifts which friends at home had sent to us, and many a charcoal fire was busy cooking wonderful dishes along the trench.

That night both sides sang carols, and the firing ended.

We had a small right-angled salient in our line, and we decided to dig a new and better trench in front to cut off the angle, and so we sallied forth one night into No Man's Land to start this work.

We waited until it was dark, and then the first party scrambled out over the parapet. A listening post crawls out in front to guard against the coming of the Hun and silently we line up where the new trench is to be dug. Just as the first party are "dressed" for digging, up goes a German star shell, and No Man's Land is as bright as Regent Street in nights of peace-time. Down we all flop until the constellation is over, and then to work. Bullets idly ping over our heads as the work proceeds, and soon our first party are down half a foot, and another party steals out and lines up on our right. Confidence soon reigns, and the earth begins to fly. Boche has not spotted us, and so the star shells are not followed by the crackle of machine guns.

After two hours the digging reliefs come out and drop into the holes already dug, whilst the first parties slip back to the trenches.

The moon comes up, but now we are getting down to our work, and a respectable parapet is rising ; and so the work goes on till dawn, when we all creep back to the trench.

Very proud we were of our first night's work and not a single casualty to report. After a night or two the trench is practically complete and we man our new line, feeling far safer in the deep, well-traversed trench, and we all are proud of our architectural feat. Have we not advanced the line and shortened it by a hundred yards ! ! The new line has to be wired, and this is more dangerous work, for we had to hammer in our wooden stakes, and you have not the consolation which the digger possesses of knowing that every minute you work you get farther under cover.

Night after night, right along the scores of miles of British front, little parties are always working on the wire—it is the least popular job in the war, but it has to be done, and the good battalion never vacates the line with gaps in the wire.

I mentioned that we had a sap within ten yards of the Germans. In reality it was a ditch with two mud walls, each wall with loopholes, one mud wall held by the Germans and one by ourselves.

This was before the days of bombs, and as one stood in the sap the garrison of the enemy could be clearly heard talking and coughing. I tried sometimes to gain some news from these gentlemen by addressing them in English, to the effect that they had far better surrender now before the vast British Armies arrived on the scene, but all I got for my trouble were guttural oaths, only a few of which I could understand. I had to visit this sap once by day and once by night for fourteen days; it was a fascinating spot, but of this more anon.

After Christmas we had to fight the elements. Our trenches, as I said, were really ditches, and here the waters began to gather. All through the night fatigue parties from the companies in rear brought hurdles and fascines, and all the time, night after night, we fought the waters. One day we would succeed in getting a dry footing all along the trench, but the rains continued and by night our temporary flooring had disappeared in the mud.

The sap was even worse, and the last few days in the line we could not get to the post without getting wet to the middle. This was an amazing midnight bath, but it is wonderful how little sickness occurs on these occasions. Many nights I lay down for an hour or two, literally soaked to the skin, and soon dropped off to sleep, and even then sleep was disturbed. This is a typical description of a night in those days.

Retire to " rest " at midnight.

12.45 a.m.  Buz—be—be—buz—buz—buz— buz . . . that beastly telephone again— perhaps it is not for me. . . . Close eyes again . . . Please, sir, Captain —— says B. Company's rations have not arrived. Ring up Head-quarters and learn that " fatigue party got lost; rations just started for trenches."

1. a.m.  Lie down again.

1.45 a.m.  Buz—be—be—buz—buz. Please, sir, telegram from Head-quarters. Message as follows :  " Brigade asks have all men received Princess Mary's gifts, and for immediate answer please."  I repeat the telegram to all companies and lie down again.

2 a.m. ⎫
2.15 a.m. ⎪
2.20 a.m. ⎬ Replies received from companies.
2.39 a.m. ⎭

2.40 a.m.  Reply sent to Battalion Head-quarters, and I lie down again.

2.57 a.m.  Adjutant wants you on the
    'phone, sir.  He cannot understand your
    message.  I reply to the adjutant and
    lie down again.
5 a.m.  Telegram from Division, sir, re-
    quiring return of gum-boots.  Return
    sent, and lie down again at 5.15.
6 a.m.  Time for stand to, sir.

No, dear reader, I did not swear.

O ye great men upon the Brigade Staff,
O ye greater men upon the Divisional
Staff, O ye wonderful great men upon the
Corps Staff, O ye amazing great men upon
the Army Staff, O ye greatest of all great
men at G.H.Q., have mercy upon the
regimental officer in the night season, and
grant him, if possible, two, three, or if
possible, four hours' sleep, so that he may
dream of châteaux and red tabs.

# CHAPTER XIII

## RICHEBOURG

WE went out for six days' rest on January 2nd, and it rained almost incessantly, so that we rather shivered at the idea of going back to our next trenches, which were in front of Richebourg, where we experienced the full power of Flanders mud.

We found that what had been trenches were now nothing but rivers, and only a few posts or " islands " were held in front, the actual firing-line troops being quartered in houses in the Rue du Bois.

On either side of the road were substantial brick cottages, which still gave good cover from the weather, and these we proceeded to fortify.

The street itself was an unhealthy spot, as we were directly enfiladed from Port Arthur away on our left, and bullets hummed along the street in some numbers, especially at night.

Here we lost an officer killed whilst visiting the sentries, and a few other casualties. We relieved the posts as frequently as possible, and half the battalion was billeted back in Richebourg, where they were busily engaged in building strong posts.

A company reported on coming out of the advanced posts that they had surprised a working party in the early morning, the fog lifting very rapidly. They were able to pour rapid fire into the Germans, and account, they think, for seven before they got back to their lines.

This company also reported two men missing. In the morning they turned up and told their story, which was that coming back from their island they thought they would use an old communication trench as there was considerable firing, and as a result one of them got bogged, and the other, who went to rescue him, also got bogged, and there they stayed all night unable to get help. In the morning they were dug out by the Irish Guards who had relieved us, and two half-frozen, blue-looking individuals limped back to billets. We wrapped them up in several blankets and sent them to hospital, but I fear they suffered severely.

From Richebourg we went back to our old line of Christmas-tide and relieved the 60th Rifles under Colonel Northey, who has since won fame in East Africa, and a sad state our old trenches were in. Here again we held the line lightly, and all relief had to be overground after dark, whilst the supports dwelt in some old farms in rear, known to us as Carlton House Terrace.

Piccadilly and Pall Mall, which we thought we had made into fine communication trenches, were now brooks, and the fascinating sap where we conversed with the Germans had been abandoned as hopeless.

The enemy was busy working on his trenches, and during this tour we got some good sniping. I got a shot at a German, but he signalled a " wash out," and disappeared. Carlton House Terrace was rather lively, and we had three men hit by a machine gun, which was evidently determined to make all suffer who patronised the " West End."

We were relieved by the 2nd Grenadiers, and it was rather an anxious relief, as the ground was white with snow and all reliefs were over the top. The old trenches had to be crossed by bridges which we had put in in the last few nights, and I remember one

company of Grenadiers had just crossed a
bridge and closed up in a field in rear of
the front trench, when a Boche searchlight
suddenly switched right on to them. For
a moment I thought their dark mass must
be discovered and ducked, expecting a hail
of bullets, as we were not more than 150
yards from the enemy, but all was quiet,
and the procession continued silently to
the front line, where man by man they slid
down to pass to their posts, whilst the Herts
as silently climbed out and marched back.

One incident I remember caused me amusement and indignation whilst in this line.
I had told all companies in the morning
that working parties should be fired on
invariably if detected. That night I was
walking round to visit the islands in the
front line, and feeling lonely—one always
feels lonely when one is by oneself at night
—when a platoon commander of ours
evidently recognised me walking in the
snow just in rear of them. To show his
ardour he ordered rapid fire on a working
party which I fear may have been imaginary;
anyhow, the effect was an immediate retort
from Hun-land in like coin, and the air was
alive with hum—zip—crack—swish, whilst
I deposited myself in a shell hole which was

two feet deep with water. The keen subaltern is sometimes rather a trial!

One had strange meetings on the occasion
of these reliefs. As I peered through the
darkness to find the officer commanding a
company of Grenadiers whom I heard coming
along the road, I suddenly found myself
face to face with a neighbour in Hertfordshire, Captain Gosselin, with whom I had
hunted and shot for many years past, but
alas, never again! for, gallant soul, he met
his death whilst tending the wounds of a
man in his company under a heavy shell
fire. My next visitor at Carlton House
Terrace, as if he had walked out of the
Carlton Club, was Captain Percy Clive, M.P.,
who to-day is on crutches, but whom all
soldiers and M.P.'s hope will soon be well.

So do those who remind one of a former
existence roll up in the snow-clad mud of
Flanders.

## CHAPTER XIV

### THE ATTACK ON THE BRICKSTACKS

TOWARDS the end of January our Colonel, Lord Hampden, left for England to command a brigade, and the responsibility now devolved on my shoulders. There was considerable liveliness in these parts, and we found ourselves on the road several days rising before dawn and marching from Hingette, where we were billeted, to points about two miles in rear of Givenchy on the La Bassée Canal, or at Essars, and there we waited all day whilst little rumours came our way about big efforts of the enemy to wrest from our troops Cuinchy and Givenchy, which are on the ridge that stops the road of the Huns to Bethune.

We learnt that the enemy had taken the brickstacks at Cuinchy, and had actually entered the village of Givenchy, to be cleared out again by the vigorous use of Welsh bayonets.

One day I received a message from Brigadier-General the Earl of Cavan, G.O.C. 4th Guards Brigade, ordering commanding officers to attend his head-quarters for a conference. Lord Cavan is one of those exceptional personalities who give confidence from the first moment you meet them, but unlike most famous generals and admirals he makes you feel his friendship at once, and you realise that you are dealing with a very human man. Short in stature, very strongly built, with a somewhat large head, he meets you with a merry twinkle in his eyes, and you find a rather unusual type of soldier, master of hounds, statesman, leader, and friend all rolled into one.

This was the first serious discussion at which I had met him. Pointing to the map he showed us where the enemy had advanced, and then said quite simply, " We will take back this culvert here, those trenches there, and then those brickstacks up to that point." Then followed instructions to each battalion and orders as to reconnaissance.

The whole description was wonderfully simple, and the orders were given in such a way that not one of us doubted they would prove successful. So it turned out,

7

for a more perfectly conceived and executed little series of operations could not be imagined.

After reminding the Guards' commanding officers that their men were very big— always a matter of pride to this little man— he dismissed us with a cheery word, and we jumped on our horses and rode back to our units, feeling that almost already the brickstacks were ours.

My impressions at the time were not that I had been listening to a great genius, but that I had been talking to a man who was full of common sense; since then, however, I have come to ask whether, after all, the greatest genius is not the man who possesses the biggest fund of that most valuable quality. How many lives would be saved if common sense always ruled, and the possible and impossible were realised by all leaders.

The brigade now moved up to the Cuinchy area, the 3rd Coldstream and Irish Guards into the line, with the Herts in close support, and the 2nd Grenadiers and 2nd Coldstream in reserve.

During the first few nights we were busily engaged in burying the dead who were lying about from the previous fighting, and the brigadier was most particular that all—British and Germans—should be carried out of the lines and buried in cemeteries in rear. It was dangerous work and trying to young hands, but we carried back across the open over a hundred dead, and gave them decent burial.

The temptation is to bury on the spot, but the disadvantages are so great that an effort is always made, if the enemy's guns permit, to carry the dead on stretchers to selected cemeteries, where great care is taken to mark and preserve the graves of the fallen.

This attack was the first occasion on which concentrated artillery was used in a surprise bombardment, and it must be remembered that, in spite of the eloquent speeches of a certain statesman, in which he assured the country that we had enough ammunition, in reality we had hardly any ammunition at all, and the enemy pounded us all day whilst we were unable to reply.

On this occasion Lord Cavan and our Divisional General, Major General Horne, the famous gunner who now commands the 1st Army, had managed to get quite a formidable array of heavies, and for those days a considerable amount of ammunition. Our guns were all concentrated so as to bring converging fire to bear on the objective, which was only about half a mile wide, and the heavies opened a deliberate fire during the morning upon the Boche positions.

There were noises new to us, as 9-inch and 15-inch shells moaned their way over our heads, and the dull roar of their explosions followed in quick succession. Now the 60-pounders gave tongue with a sharp crack, and the field howitzers, with unassuming voice, joined in the chorus.

Our battalion lay in wait just under the Cuinchy ridge, and at midday I had orders to move two companies up. They moved across the open in artillery formation, and as I watched them go forward, the enemy's shrapnel was playing freely round them, but each little group pressed on until they reached the village and passed from sight. At 2 p.m. the whole of our artillery commenced intense gun fire, and all around us the field guns joined in with sharp angry barks, whilst the whistle, swish, and groan of shells of all calibres filled the air with noise.

On these occasions I always have an intense desire to sleep—the din affects one in such a manner that one's eyes almost inevitably close.

Climbing to the top of the roof of my quarters I could now see columns of what looked like red smoke—the dust of the brickstacks—mixing with the black and white of the incessant explosions, and rising in the air.

At 2.15 the Irish Guards and Coldstream assaulted and rushed the enemy's trenches with the bayonet, and the Herts' supporting companies doubled forward in the rear waves with sand-bags, tools, and ammunition. Guardsmen could be seen chasing Germans round the brickstacks, and in a very few minutes the whole garrison were either dead or captured, whilst the attackers proceeded to consolidate.

The booty—machine guns, a trench mortar, stores, etc.—was sent to the rear ; and now the enemy began to hate us with his guns, but it was too late, for the whole operation was completed.

The two little attacks of the preceding day had also come off, and Lord Cavan's plans had succeeded in every particular; losses had been inflicted on the enemy, our casualties were slight, and we had got every yard we set out to win.

Our lads came back that night after their first journey across No Man's Land, laden with the spoils of war in the shape of helmets, rifles, and bayonets, and most of them smoking German cigars.

One of our companies remained in some support trenches, and were heavily shelled. During this shelling two Herts stretcher-bearers were sent for to convey a wounded man out. As they ran down the trench a shell knocked in the parapet and half buried them both; one was wounded with a shrapnel bullet in his side, and the other in the ear. It was suggested that they should hand over their job to others, but they insisted that they should carry on, as the patient was badly wounded, and carried him out to the village, where the man died and the two gallant lads were found in a state of collapse. Both these men were awarded the Russian Medal which our Allies grant to the very brave.

Next day we were ordered up to support again, and one of our companies arrived in the Coldstream line just in time to have a shoot at a feeble counter-attack, which was driven off by the fire from our trenches.

We had not taken a major part in these operations, but had nevertheless been "blooded," and we were proud to receive

a message from the G.O.C. Division addressed
to the Brigadier, that

He had received with unqualified satis-
faction the report of the steady, soldier-like
bearing under heavy fire of the 1st Battalion
Hertfordshire Regiment (T.F.), both in support of the attack on February 6th, and again
during the bombardment on the afternoon
of the following day.

Now we worked like beavers, and concentrated our efforts on a long communication trench, which is famous in those parts
as Hertford Street, and which we hope has
saved many a valuable life for England.

.      .      .      .      .

We had advanced our position, and consequently had got ahead of the French, who
joined us on the La Bassée Road; so on
February 14th, they attacked on our right,
to come level, and we got a good view of
them as they went over.  At first we thought
they had captured their trench, but at
the time this had not occurred, and a
French officer who went through our right
trenches after dark, with Captain Clive of
the Grenadiers and Major Fowke of the
R.E., had a surprising adventure.

They crossed the La Bassée Road and

entered the German trench, walking along
until they came to some German equipment.
A little further on they found a dugout lit
up, and looking in, saw Germans. A sharp
challenge in German by a sentry caused them
to beat a hurried retreat, accompanied by
bullets, and it thus transpired that the
small French attacking force had been overwhelmed after entering the trench.

A subsequent French attack brought them
level and included in our lines the famous
mill which months after we got to know very
well.

# CHAPTER XV

## GIVENCHY

THE 4th Guards Brigade, after the attack at Cuinchy, settled down to improve the line, and everywhere we sapped forward and joined the saps, thus advancing the line. The Herts went into the left of the Givenchy sector, which was a very interesting part of the front, for here we were on the extreme northern edge of the high ground, and our trench line ran down what is known as the Bluff to the flat land which runs right away north.

On our left was a gap of some 600 yards between us and the La Plantin sector, which at this time was held by another brigade; there was therefore a regular crescent in the line, and to us was allotted the task of making a breastwork right out in the open in this wide stretch of No Man's Land. This was the more exciting, as the German trenches were absolutely in line with our trenches on the Givenchy front, and looking down,

off our Bluff we actually commanded the
top of their trenches for several miles, a
fact which upsets another war theory, for
it is now proved that where trenches are
sufficiently traversed, enfilade firing of Infantry, at any rate, cannot turn you out.

Our plan was to build a breastwork up
in the open and to go in a straight line towards the Germans on our left, the idea
being ultimately to capture the German front
line and thus straighten the crescent. Now
to build a breastwork within a few hundred
yards of the enemy is not an easy task, and
very different to digging a trench, but we
decided to start by making sand-bag forts
with gaps between, so that in case of necessity we could occupy the forts prior to an
attack, even though the breastwork was
not finished.

The first night was simple, for after elabor-
ate preparations we carried out 1,000 filled
sand-bags and had a working party in No
Man's Land filling others. When dawn
came, therefore, fifty yards from our left
there appeared a magnificent erection of
brand new sand-bag work which greatly
delighted us and annoyed Fritz, who proceeded to shell the fort during the day,
although it was unoccupied.

The next night we proceeded to make another fort fifty yards on, and with reliefs all through the night another substantial edifice appeared at dawn.

We had now progressed 100 yards in the direction of the enemy, so he became still more savage, and we quite realised that during the next night he would probably be very busy with artillery and machine guns laid on the spot where the third fort would appear fifty yards farther on, so we decided to get our men out directly after dark, carry all our material with us, and jump 100 yards, and this artifice proved successful, for whereas our men were working all night long within 100 yards of that section of the German trench which was on our left, they were shelling and sweeping with machine guns the interval where they expected us to be.

The brigade on our left by now were making substantial progress with the breast-work which was coming forward to meet ours, and after a time we had filled all the gaps and had a continual line of breastworks, and were heartily congratulated on completing our difficult and dangerous task.

One night, another battalion, fresh out from England, was attached to us for in-

struction, and so we put them on to build
breastwork in No Man's Land by way of
introducing them to war; and as there was
a good deal of shell fire knocking about, which
is rather alarming to new troops, they were,
I think, rather pleased, when the German fire
became intense, to be ordered back to the
trenches. As it was pitch-dark and no
talking was allowed, our officers and non-
commissioned officers had rather a difficulty
in collecting the party, all of whom had been
ordered to lie flat during the shelling, and
a subaltern told me a rather amusing story
about how he discovered one of our sergeants
haranguing a London soldier on the ground.
"Get up," he said, "you lazy Cockney.
Do you think I am going to stand about
here all night getting you fellows in?"
As the Cockney, in the darkness of the night,
apparently refused to budge, the sergeant,
growing emphatic, gave the offender a kick;
and still finding no response, he stooped
down and discovered he had been addressing
a dead cow.

Another good story is told in connection
with this breastwork. A battalion fresh
from home took over the line, and the first
night a large party was told off to carry
hurdles, etc., across country to where the

breastwork was being completed. There was a bright moon, and the troops in the line were not occupying the breastwork; but as the party approached they saw figures walking about on our side of the breastwork, whereupon the party lay down and opened rapid fire, and messages were sent back to say that the enemy had broken through the line. It was only an hour later that it was discovered that the imagined intruders were our own sappers waiting for the party, and they had managed to escape this murderous and enthusiastic fire by crawling along a very shallow trench to our own line on the right.

The Brigadier told me how he had heard the alarming news, and I asked him what he did? " Oh," he replied, " I mounted my servant as a sentry; but I had heard these stories so often that I was not unduly alarmed! "

## CHAPTER XVI

### MORTARS AND MINES

DURING our stay in this sector we made great strides in the art of trench mortars, and by begging, borrowing, stealing, and sometimes indenting, we succeeded in collecting quite a number of what were known as gas-pipes. They were very rough-and-ready trench mortars: simply a circular metal tube with a couple of legs in front to make them sit up and a little hole at the bottom through which to put a fuse. Through the hole was poured a little powder and a few inches of fuse; down the tube is dropped a home-made bomb, the fuse is lit, the operators run for their lives, and suddenly there is a loud thut, and the bomb is clearly observed going high into the air until it drops in the neighbourhood of trenches, preferably German. Shortly after this there is a loud explosion, and if the shot is a lucky one, all sorts of interesting things are seen to be elevated. These primitive weapons had their disadvantages, for frequently they burst, and then, if the mortar team had not absented themselves, there was trouble. In addition to this, they called down special hate of the enemy, who would carefully mark the spot from which the mortar was fired and then concentrate a battery on the spot.

.        .        .        .        .

The result of this was that the mortar guns which were manned by our own men became somewhat unpopular with the Infantry, and we could only console them by reminding them how much they disliked German mortars. The moment the " thut " of our mortar guns was heard, we could hear the enemy blowing horns and whistles, with a view to warning the garrison, who thus were able to see the direction in which our bombs were going to fall and clear out of the way. We therefore adopted new tactics, by which at a given signal we fired some twenty mortars on a one-mile front simultaneously, and in co-operation with the late Major Trefusis commanding the Irish Guards (who was promoted Brigadier-General prior to his being killed in this very

sector some months later) we organised
many of these mortar strafes.

.     .     .     .     .

About this time mining activity became
more general, and we had frequent alarums
and excursions in this connection. Mining
activity, which is continuous on large sectors
of the front, always keeps troops in the
neighbourhood on tenter-hooks, and many
are the reports which come from companies
in the front line to the effect that the enemy
can be heard working underneath them.
This usually turns out to be some one digging
in a deep dug-out in our own lines. The
object of mining is of course to get under
your enemy's trenches and to blow him, and
in order to prevent this, countermining
takes place. When the enemy miners are
heard, we mine in their direction, and try
and blow him before he blows us. It is
the least spectacular form of warfare, but
it demands great courage and endurance on
the part of the miners, for when the enemy
blows his mine, even if our shaft is not
wrecked, the occupants are liable to be
asphyxiated by fumes.

The first indication that you have of
a mine being blown is a great rocking
sensation like an earthquake, immediately

after which a dull roar is heard and tons of earth are thrown into the air, forming a crater, sometimes 50 to 150 feet wide. When a mine is heard it is always an anxious moment, whilst we wonder whether the enemy has succeeded in getting under our line, although frequently he blows in No Man's Land, with a view to occupying the crater either for offensive or defensive purposes.

The side which fires the mine obviously has the great advantage in occupying the crater, as they are all prepared; and if the intrusion is too embarrassing to the defenders' trenches, a counter-attack has to be made at once in order to get possession of the crater.

As a matter of fact, in many parts of the line the Germans and ourselves each hold their own lip of the crater, and it is death to either to show themselves. In these spots hand-bombing is of course a continual attraction.

In this same sector, some months after I had left my regiment, the following incident took place. An advanced post was held by a platoon of thirty-five men, and the Germans opposite them had become very active, whereupon Lieut. - Colonel

Page,[1] my successor in command of the Herts, decided that he would withdraw the garrison temporarily whilst the enemy's work was thoroughly shelled. The garrison were accordingly withdrawn, and within five minutes the work which they had held was blown by an enemy mine.

But for this extraordinary coincidence there is little doubt that the whole garrison would have been killed.

Other corps have been less fortunate, and at times mining on both sides must have inflicted severe casualties, but on the whole, our miners always felt that they were superior to their antagonists under ground, just as the Infantry are superior on the top.

[1] Colonel Page, who commanded the battalion for eighteen months, was killed at St. Julian in the great attack of July 31st, 1917.

# CHAPTER XVII

## NEUVE CHAPELLE

On February 10th, at 4.30 a.m. the brigade was in reserve for the offensive at Neuve Chapelle. In order to arrive at our rendezvous we left Bethune at about 2 a.m. and marched to Le Preol, where we rested beside La Bassée Canal. Just as we were arriving at this spot we could hear the roar of the guns as the intense bombardment heralded the attack. The sound was just like continuous thunder, and one could not help contrasting—for war is all contrasts—the peaceful spot where we settled down to wait with the inferno which was raging a few miles off.

Whilst we were waiting and expecting every moment to be ordered to take our share in the proceedings, various scraps of news came through to us, and we heard of the great success of the original attack on the line and of prisoners being marched

to the rear, and we realised that a turning
point had come in the war, for up to now
neither side had really succeeded in storming any considerable line of trenches.

At Neuve Chapelle the tactics of Cuinchy
were adopted on a larger scale, viz. the surprise attack after an intense concentrated
bombardment; but once again the British
Army was to learn the lesson of the extraordinary power of machine guns well placed.
During the main attack at Neuve Chapelle
our division was making a subsidiary attack
on Givenchy, and there the 1st 60th, 2nd
South Staffords, and the 1st King's made
a very gallant attempt with small artillery
support to capture the Bluff and the high
ground just north of the La Bassée Canal.
Four times the South Staffords entered the
German front trench, but four times were
driven out by machine guns. The King's
reached the German wire, which they could
not penetrate, and the 60th, who entered
the German trench in the only place
where the wire was cut, could not maintain
their hold. At night on the first day of
Neuve Chapelle we marched back again
to billets, and the next day marched to
Givenchy, where we relieved the sorely
tried 6th Brigade, whilst the attack,

away on our left, progressed a little farther.

It is never a cheery job taking over trenches from battalions which have just received a knock; and besides being somewhat heavily shelled, we were busily engaged after dark trying to rescue wounded in No Man's Land; and three nights after the attack one of our company sergeant-majors went out to the German wire and brought back on his back a wounded corporal of the K.R.R. The next night we succeeded in bringing in two more wounded men of the same corps who had lain out there four days and four nights.

The net result of Neuve Chapelle was, that the 1st Army made the biggest bag of prisoners since the war of position had started, and had shown that with careful artillery preparation the German front system, at any rate, could be carried. We had also learnt once again in this subsidiary attack that little can be gained by attacking an enemy position whilst the wire remains intact.

# CHAPTER XVIII

## SPRING

WITH the drying of the ground work proceeded apace, and we very soon turned the Cuinchy and Givenchy sectors into a really first-class system of trenches, and our casualties, which had been heavy when we first entered the line, were rapidly decreasing as we deepened, traversed, and perfected our line. My head-quarters for three weeks were at a famous spot known as Windy Corner, in rear of Givenchy, and two or three times a day the enemy artillery searched the village. In the farm next to our head-quarters an unlucky shell pitched right in the doorway, mortally wounding four men, and another shell penetrated our roof, but on the whole we were extremely lucky, especially as in one day, March 19th, the enemy fired no less than 2,000 heavy shells in our neighbourhood, a large proportion of which fell around the ruins of Givenchy Church.

During the afternoon I was walking up to
the line and watching German 8-inch shells
bursting on Givenchy, sending up clouds
of brick-dust and hurling their debris considerable distances, when I heard one shell
coming towards the church, which was a
quarter of a mile from where I stood, and
was astonished, instead of hearing it burst,
to hear a terrific humming noise and to see
the shell coming straight in my direction.
As I lay flat on the ground it came buzzing
like an enormous bee, and fell with a thud
in the ground twenty yards from where I
lay.

This was a " dud " shell which had
pitched on the hill at Givenchy and had
ricochetted in my direction, but happily,
being a " dud " it did not explode when it
reached my neighbourhood, to my intense
relief.

The normal trench life proceeded, and a
few yards from my house was the British
cemetery which, when we first came, con-
tained only a dozen graves, but which, before
we left those parts, stretched over an acre
of ground. Every day the chaplain would
come up and men of different regiments
would be reverently conveyed to their graves,
which were beautifully kept and marked

with various descriptions of wooden crosses
and little metal plates attached, with the
name, number, and regiment clearly marked
thereon. These cemeteries are eventually
wired round, and the whole work is now
carried out with great care.

. . . . .

Every day, these spring mornings, aeroplanes would circle overhead, and sentries
were posted at intervals to warn the men
billeted in the villages when a German was
in the heavens. Daily you could see our
aeroplanes going far over the German lines,
hunted all the way by what looked like
little white puffs of smoke—in reality, bursting shrapnel—and frequently you could see
a plane with fifty white puffs stretching
out behind it where the wind had not yet
dispersed the smoke of the bursting shrapnel.
Now the ordinary Infantry man knows
that a German shell is not intended for him,
and consequently he thinks it is merely bad
luck when they pitch in his direction; but
for the airman it is different, for every one
of those innocent puffs means 200 shrapnel
bullets intended for him individually, and
therein lies the great difference in the out-
look of the man in the air as opposed to the
man on the ground.

It is a remarkable thing, when frequently thousands of shells are fired into the air in the course of the day, that there are not many casualties as a result of the falling fragments. The pieces come down with a humming noise, and strange as it may seem, these hummings are regarded with great contempt by every one who hears them. In reality, of course, they are coming down about the same pace as the shell goes up, so that if they do hit you, you are likely to know all about it. In all my long time in the trenches I only saw one mishap of this description, and that was when we were lazily sitting outside a billet a mile behind the line in the sun, and watching one of our planes circling over the enemy's trenches. We could hear distant enemy rifle fire aimed against the plane, and a man in my regiment was walking along the road towards us when all of a sudden he fell. It transpired that a bullet had entered the nape of his neck and gone right through his body and out at his heel, and he died as the result of his wounds. This, however, was an exceptional case, and I am reminded of the philosophy of a private in my company when I first went to France, who told me that " there was far more air about than

lead." We decided, however, to make the
life of the German airman as uncomfortable
as possible, and so whenever he came low
over our lines we opened rapid fire upon
him, but although this was very uncomfortable for the airman, I must confess that
beyond keeping him up high I never saw
damage inflicted upon him ; the only time
that I saw an airman forced to descend by
fire from trenches was when a Lewis gun
got in a lucky shot and forced him to descend
behind the German lines.

.        .        .        .        .

Whilst we were in the Givenchy sector
we were pestered by German field artillery,
which was very active. The guns have a
low trajectory, and if you are being fired
at, and happen to be in the way, you do
not hear them coming, " whiz—bang " being
heard almost simultaneously, and then you
are lucky if you are only covered with earth.
These shells do remarkably little harm, although sometimes a direct hit on the parapet
with percussion will play mischief, and then
men get buried. On one occasion in this
tour I was walking round a traverse, and a
shell burst in the next bay. A scared man
ran round the traverse, and I asked him if

any one was hurt ?   " Bill may be," he said,
but Bill could not be found, so I gave the
order to dig, and we dug Bill out just in
time, and respiration brought him back to
life and hope.

Shrapnel shows discrimination.  I was
once walking up a trench between two men
much shorter than myself when a shell
burst straight in front of us, and both my
attendants were hit, whilst I went unscathed.

# CHAPTER XIX

## THE BATTLE OF FESTUBERT

EARLY in May there were whisperings of liveliness in Flanders, and subtle rumour made the round of trench and billet. These rumours usually come from England, where somebody's wife has heard that a big push is coming off, and as she, in confidence, invariably tells somebody else's wife, eventually in spite of the imperative necessity of secrecy, these rumours are spread all through England and thence to France.

On May 6th, the whole of the 4th Guards Brigade was in line holding from the La Bassée Road to Le Plantin, and on May 8th, at 4.45 a.m., the British artillery commenced a great bombardment on our left, which was taken up by the French artillery on our right.

I went to the top of a high building, and there I could see the whole of the ground between Givenchy and Neuve Chapelle where the attack was to take place.

Hundreds of shells could be seen bursting along the German line every minute, and the whole world seemed to vibrate with the sounds of hell. Immediately to our right the French " 75 " guns were adding their music, " thud, thud, thud, thud " in quick succession, until all the south was thudding its chorus.

Just before the bombardment commenced in the dim light of dawn a British aeroplane was seen returning over the lines, flying low under fire, when, to the horror of all our men, it burst into flames and dived to earth in No Man's Land, and all those who look for signs and portents wagged their heads.

At 5.40 a.m. the attack commenced, and British and French left their trenches to the north and south of us respectively. The British attack had the effect of a right wheel, and the French a left wheel, and we were the first pivot of each attack, and stood firm whilst we hoped the attacks would progress so as to envelop La Bassée opposite us.

Directly the attack began, all our five battalions opened rapid fire on the German trenches, the idea being to prevent the machine guns opposite us bringing flanking fire to bear on the attackers and to hold the enemy reserves opposite us.

From the Herts trenches the French bayonets could be seen glittering in the sun as their long waves of attackers advanced, and then we longed for news, which seems to take ages to filter through on such occasions.

Soon we heard that the attack immediately on our left by the 1st Division had been held up by wire, but that the 4th Corps away to the north was progressing well, and the French were getting on.

Reports now came through of German troops concentrating at La Bassée and Violaines opposite us, and remembering the passion of the enemy for attacking at the junction of the French and British armies, we ardently prayed for a counter-attack, which never came. In the afternoon we learnt that the French had captured trenches opposite Loos, and—a great triumph—they had wrested from the Hun the vital spur of Notre Dame de Lorette. The British 1st Division, we heard, had tried again, but once more the wire had defeated them.

We were in a kind of backwater where all was calm, whilst the rushing torrents of war were surging to either side of us, and so we sat warming ourselves in the sun,

just as if we were in some land of peace
whilst thousands of men were fighting and
dying within a mile or so on either side of us.

Not a shell was fired at us, and as night
descended we listened to the distant roar,
and each man wondered, "Are we too for
it?"

# CHAPTER XX

## ON THE EDGE OF THE BATTLE

WE soon heard, for on May 13th we were relieved by the 1st Division, and the Camerons took over the line held by the Herts. The 1st Brigade had been very badly mauled in their attacks, and had left many gallant Highlanders behind; and as we knew that we were going to march to that same place from whence they came, their news was not too cheery.

We marched to Le Touret, where we lay down in a field which was allotted to us for a bivouac. The next day we were given buildings for billets, which pleased us as the nights were cold, and we then heard that the attack of the previous Sunday, which had failed, was to be reattempted. And so the usual joke went round. "They 'ad ter send for us Guards," says a Hertfordshire Territorial. "Whenever there's a job as no one else can tackle, they wires for the blooming old 2nd Division. Serves the 'Uns right, says I."

This was Saturday, May 14th, and for us nothing doing, so I rode away to the rear, where the harsh bark of the guns becomes a muffled boom; there where the sun poured out its joyous warmth for the fields and the trees to bathe in, where birds sing and children play.

So we rode through villages and over fields, a friend and I, and we might have been away back in Hertfordshire.

Guardsmen were billeted in several of the villages, and cheering could be heard as terrific games of football progressed. What a strange race we are! Look at those hulking giant babies, rushing for goal whilst comrades cheer; and to-morrow they will rush again, when all will play, and none will be spectators. Then, too, men will fall in the mud—yes, men will fall in the mud.

.        .        .        .        .

Back to Le Touret, and what a different scene! From dusk until 10.30 p.m. the troops who were to attack early on the morrow marched along the main road past our little cottage. It is good to be a Briton when British troops march to the attack. No band here; no cheering crowds; but

9

song : the kind of songs we often hear when
troops at night are marching back to rest,
but the singing is less harsh—there is more
music, or so it seems. They see us watching
them go by, and there is just a touch of
swagger, just a half smile, for they know
that the spectators are asking themselves
how many of the songsters will come back
by that road; they know in this hour they
are British. That is why they swagger, and
that is why they sing and smile.

More troops and more—English, Scottish,
Welsh, and Irish—on they go; and now night,
with its quiet hours, is here, and so singing
must stop or the enemy will shell the roads.

We heard quips and jokes, and more
battalions move by with the same unequalled
look of the British regular army. Many
battalions marched by who had caught it
at Mons, at Le Cateau and the Aisne, who
had got it in the neck at Ypres, who knew
their modern war; but although there were
many there fresh from the depots, there were
none who had failed to win the spirit of the
great dead, who in dying had stopped the
barbarian hordes and saved Calais, Havre,
and perhaps the world.

. . . . .

The 4th Guards Brigade were now warned

as Corps Reserve, and at 11.30 p.m. the attack commenced, and messages came through to say that the 5th and 6th Brigades, both of our division, had gained ground and captured trenches.

At 2.45 a.m. the terrific noise of our guns hailed a second attack, and I ran outside, to see the heavens splashed with what looked like continuous lightning, whilst field guns cracked and barked their unearthly chorus and heavies moaned and purred their way over our heads from miles behind; then scores of German star shells lit the land, and great events we knew were happening.

At 3.25, suddenly sprays of white stars proclaimed the fact that the 7th Division had gained their objective on the right, and we knew it was time for breakfast, for we were veterans enough now to remember that no man can fight on an empty stomach, and soon the whole battalion was drawing on the cookers.

A disturbed night this, which is a pity, for who can tell if there is sleep for the Herts for the next few days ?

.     .     .     .     .

A day of sensation it turned out, for soon our road was a continuous picture of interest. Artillery limbers trotting up with ammunition, and empty limbers with sweating horses galloping back for more; Red Cross motors moving down the road gently with their burdens; groups of wounded men walking back chaffing and joking; this one with a blood-stained bandage round his head, another with his coat ripped open and shoulder bound; here is one limping between two bandaged comrades; there is a lad, very young and very pale, but he waves a German helmet and laughs—then faints beside the road.

Shells begin to crack in the neighbourhood, but nobody seems disturbed, least of all a fair-haired boy who has a word for all, as they limp to Blighty. All guess his identity, and as they pass on we hear them say, " Some Prince, that ! "

Now we see a surging crowd of Tommies rush into the road, and there round the corner come grey figures, prisoners to join the procession on the highway. They pass, ten or twenty at a time, with two or three Tommies with fixed bayonets, who look as if they have suddenly heard that some distant aunt had left them fortunes.

One does not expect prisoners to look pleased, but it is not a good type of face this. Some of them, it is true, are better, but most

have the look of the man in the dock—the
man who before you have heard the evidence
possesses the look of guilt.

Be careful, my friends, in believing that
the Kaiser alone is bad, for the vast majority
of these Prussians possess the face of a
brute.

## CHAPTER XXI

### " THE GUARDS ARE FOR IT "

WE now heard that Canadians were expected to arrive in the area, and I walked along the road to meet them. So far Canadians had not come our way, and we had only heard the fine story of how they stood firm in the great gas attack at Ypres.

Soon the head of a column comes in view, the Canadian Highland Brigade, and here they are, the cousins from over the pond who have come thousands of miles to do their bit. There I recognise, riding at the head of their men, bankers and merchants of Toronto, Real Estate agents and others who have forgotten all that dollars mean, left the wheat pits and the town plots, who have forsaken the building of a nation to save the fabric of Empire. On they came, hundreds and thousands, marching along with a swing and the look of men who have " been there." Fine fellows these, and it is

something to know that if we bite the dust
the Canadians will be behind us to carry
on.

.     .     .     .     .

Lord Cavan calls a hurried conference of
commanding officers at the Herts head-
quarters, and orders are given that the
Grenadiers and Irish Guards will take over
the captured German trenches, the Herts
will be in support, and the 2nd and 3rd Coldstream in reserve. The brigade was to
attack the line Ferme Cœur D'Avoigne—
Quinque Rue. We fell out by the side of
the road in Le Touret and waited for the
Grenadiers and Irish to pass.

Soon they came, marching at that stately
stride which denotes the Guards, and we
throw and catch cheery words from our
comrades of many months as they swing
by, looking the embodiment of all that
is perfect in the fighting man. Sometimes,
Londoners, you may wonder at all the little
tricks of drill and footwork as you watch
the Guards in Birdcage Walk, and when you
see the harsh discipline sometimes you ask,
is it not overdone ? No, a thousand times
no, for if you saw your pipe-clayed polished
Guards in the field you would know that it
is just that discipline which makes the

supreme fighting man who is the pride of your army.

Again we ask the question, How many of these great cheery giants will come out of the crucible? and almost we forget that we, too, are part of the show when we see these friends of ours marching to the end of the world.

The last of the Irish are passing; a whistle blows, and the Herts fall in; a second whistle, and every rifle is sloped; a third, and the whole battalion steps out in column, joining up with that very gallant company on the road—the long, long road to the Rhine.

Soon we leave the road for the fields, as German woolies (5·9 high-explosive shrapnel) are cracking over our heads like last trumps, so we move quickly into artillery formation as the march continues.

We halt at last in some support trenches, and here we are to wait for orders. There had been lots of rain, and our trenches were nothing but muddy ditches; and now the rain came down in torrents as we tried to settle down to rest; but if you attempted to lie on the ground you sunk into two inches of watery mud, so there was nothing for it but to cut out little seats, and thus we waited for night and sat sleepless whilst the torrent poured on us till dawn, and we listened for news from the front.

.        .        .        .        .

The plan was that the Irish Guards should make a frontal attack on the farm Cœur D'Avoigne, the Grenadiers on their right taking the farm in flank. One company of the Herts was ordered to attack on the left of the Irish Guards, and the remaining three companies to be ready to support either of the attacking battalions.

The attack intended originally for dawn was postponed until 9 a.m., and then to 4.30 p.m. Meanwhile our attacking company moved up just in rear of the Irish Guards, and we marched up behind breastworks just in rear of them. All day the Germans shelled the trenches with heavies, and when I went to see our forward company they were sitting with very little cover whilst shells were falling with loud crumps all round them, but just not on them. Whilst I had a hurried conversation with the company commander a shell exploded in a cottage 200 yards away, and a mass of black smoke, mingled with red brick-dust, belched upwards, and crash in all directions went

bricks, timber, and earth.  When the dust
cleared there was no cottage left.

. . . . .

The Canadians now came up behind us,
and at 4.20 p.m. a ten minutes' bombardment
of intense character, a terrific reply from
the Germans, and then the attack was
launched.  I moved up to see what was
happening, and streams of wounded Irish
Guardsmen began to trail back—a sickening
sight for supporting troops—and I found
myself up in our old salient of Christmas,
in ground I knew.  The noise was now
terrific, so that there might have been a
thousand devils loose in the air, when a
messenger of the Irish Guards rushed up
to me and asked if I had seen the commanding officer.  " No," I replied.

" Then, sir," he said, " I report to you.
All our officers are hit, and I have been sent
back here to report for orders."

" How far have you advanced ? " I queried.

" Three hundred yards from behind the
German trench, and absolutely held up by
machine guns."

I could not find Major Trefusis the
C.O., and feared he was hit, so I decided
to reinforce with one company, which
happened to be my old company from

my native town, and in twenty minutes they appeared and I sent them over the top. Every man I knew well as they came by me in the trench whilst Irish Guards were filtering back to the dressing station, bleeding and reeling, and Irish Guards were lying dead across the bottom of the trench, but not a man of ours faltered, and many a joke was cracked for my edification as they formed up. Then over they went, and machine gun bullets began to tap, tap, tap, around.

Now I was in the old German trench, and there to my delight I found Trefusis— bravest of souls—alive, cool, and deliberate, so we discussed the situation, and I told him that I had been ordered to relieve his battalion after dark.

There, out in front of us, was the khaki line all lying flat and gradually digging in on the ground as they lay.

We now made plans for the relief, and I got back to the salient where my head-quarters were by now established. Herts wounded were beginning to come back, and on a stretcher I espied a man who had served under me many years in time of peace. He was the wag of the company, and his waggishness led several times to slight insubordination, and he had appeared before me at orderly room.

Now, as he lay face down on the stretcher and saw me, a roguish look entered his eyes and his pale face lit up as he said, " Well, sir, I shan't worry you any more; that will be a relief to you at orderly room." I saw he was in frightful pain, and I confess to a prayer that he might be spared to cause me endless orderly rooms. I remembered that half an hour before I had heard him cheering on his mates with ridiculous jokes as he climbed over the top.

It is instructive to see how the bad boys of the family often shine in war—this is only one good reason why we should not judge too freely when we thank God we are not as other men.

.    .    .    .    .

The net result of the attack was that the Grenadiers, Irish Guards, and our company of Herts had advanced 300 yards beyond the German trenches, where further progress was hopeless as the ground in front was a glacis which was swept by machine gun fire.

Our company on the left had, with a machine gun of the Irish Guards, progressed farthest; and Major Page of the Herts, with twenty men, actually got on about 200 yards farther—quite close to the objective; but finding himself in the air and isolated, came back in line with the advanced attackers when it was clear that no support could reach him.

The remnants of the attackers, reinforced by two more Herts platoons, dug in in the open in front of the enemy, and refused to budge an inch as they gradually burrowed their way underground.

## CHAPTER XXII

### NIGHT

DIRECTLY dark came I went out with two fresh companies and sited the new line, and got them to work with pick and shovel. Meanwhile the battlefield had to be cleared. Dead and wounded were lying about all over the ground.

All night long our stretcher bearers and volunteers from the spare companies were searching for wounded, and here a voice calling in the night and there a groan guided the good Samaritans who laboured on through the long hours until every single wounded man had been conveyed back to safety. Meanwhile the digging went on unceasingly in reliefs, because we knew that unless we could dig in by dawn, hell was in store for us. Just as dawn was coming the protecting screen was brought in, and the trench was down, all along the 350-yards front, to an average depth of four feet, and magnificently traversed.

It was a grand piece of work by men who had had no sleep for two days and nights, who had been drenched to the skin and been under incessant shell fire; and well it was, for, but for that great night's work, few would have survived the shelling which dawn was to bring.

All that day the new trench was shelled by 5·9 high explosives, and for hours the deafening crack went on as the green and white fumes burst and rolled away in woolly clouds.

We were all fatigued, and any moment we expected a counter-attack, till at last the hour approached for our relief by the 2nd Coldstream at dusk. As it got dark, however, the Germans redoubled their efforts, and such was the barrage that for over two hours the Coldstream had to wait before they could approach the trenches.

A corporal coming out from the front line, dazed and shaken, told how he was the last of his company, but I found out that high explosives had wiped out fourteen men to his right and left, and he had crawled back, hardly knowing where he was or what had happened.

That day's shelling cost us sixty casualties in our new trench, and with these added to

our losses of the day before, we left the line
with the loss of six officers and 124 other
ranks, of whom twenty-two were killed.
During the last twenty-four hours our
stretcher bearers had dressed no less than
300 wounded men of our own and the Irish,
and carried more than 100 stretcher cases a
mile back to the dressing station. Those
who know can realise the kind of ground
we had to work in, pitted with craters and
oozing with mud, and will I think agree
that this is no mean feat.

The fatigue of that night was great. I
had a sprained ankle, and could hardly keep
awake on my horse as I rode back, and how
much more my men must have suffered
from exhaustion I can only guess.

We were a very weary crowd on relief,
but we were proud, for, as our general told
us later, we had done all that soldiers could
do. We had advanced our line, we had dug
in in face of the enemy in daylight, and we
had stayed there under a shelling which had
tested to top strain the sticking power of
human beings.

.        .        .        .        .

The following day we marched to Bethune,
and the next to Labeuvriere, a charming
village with many trees all green with early

foliage, a brook to bathe in, and woods through which to roam at will and forget. Our quarters were in a delightful old convent with a shaded garden, where we spread ourselves lengthwise on the lawn and got our news of how the Canadians carried on in the land we had left.

A church parade and complimentary words from Major-General Horne, commanding the division, battalion drills and practising wood fighting, with alfresco concerts in the convent garden at night—all tended to bring us back to fighting form. Give Tommy pleasant surroundings, and he soon recovers from any ordeal.

## CHAPTER XXIII

### THE MINING DISTRICT

AFTER a delightful rest the brigade marched to Nœux les Mines, an inhabited mining village, where we took over from the French reserves. I had a nice little house for my head-quarters, and had just settled down in a deck-chair on the equally nice garden when a German shell took a piece out of the garden wall. It was not meant for the garden, but for the cross-roads 100 yards beyond, so it was no good worrying—probably an enemy aeroplane had seen the brigade on the march. After that the Boche lengthened, and we were less disturbed.

St. Andrew's Day demanded a banquet of Old Etonians, and some sixty of the old school in the brigade sat down to a magnificent spread in the Hotel de Ville. Our Brigadier and all five commanding officers were there to sing the old songs which Lord Cavan led with a will, and after dinner

the subalterns danced together whilst we
old gentlemen wended our way home to
our billets.

.    .    .    .    .

From Nœux les Mines we marched to
Annequin, and the brigade took over the
line south of the La Bassée road; and here
we advanced the whole line by digging forward so that No Man's Land by Hohenzollern
redoubt was reduced by a hundred yards.

.    .    .    .    .

Soon we had what was for us, sad news,
that Lord Cavan, under whom we had
served since we came to France, was off to
command a division. He was succeeded in
command of the brigade by Colonel Geoffrey
Fielding, who was an old friend, as he had
commanded the 3rd Coldstream all these
months.

Back we went to the Givenchy line again,
and here we were busily engaged in making
breastworks in front of Le Plantin, and for
some time the 2nd Division remained in
these parts improving the line.

.    .    .    .    .

Resting at Le Quesnoy we had a grand
sermon one day from the Bishop of Khar-
toum. Bishop Gwynne, who looks like " John

Bull," has a way with soldiers which counts,
and the happy knack of making men proud
of the part they are playing, and before he
has finished preaching you feel that not
only are you going to win the war for right
against wrong, but that you are all eventually going home to turn England into a
better, happier place than it has ever been
—surely this must be an influence for good.

# CHAPTER XXIV

## BOMBING

WE were getting very expert in the use of hand grenades, and a large proportion of the battalion had learnt the use of the bombs which were now handed out. Our bombers were the heroes of the battalion, and some of them became quite famous for their skill.

Bombing was no joke in the early days, as many accidents occurred and casualties were unhappily frequent, because no perfect bomb had been invented. Two gallant young Guards officers, who were the bombing instructors of the brigade, had lost their lives during instruction. One of them was killed by a bomb exploding in his pupil's hand not a hundred yards from where I stood.

These accidents were a great worry, as the moral effect was bad, but I am glad to say that officers were always ready to take a class within an hour of a fatal accident, and the work was carried on.

When we started we used jam tins, and as the bomb was of local manufacture, the dangers were always great ; one thing, however, was clear, and that was that trenches had recently been lost by the enemy bombing our people out, and the only way to beat bombs was by bombs, so we all put our minds to this matter.

The " Batty " bomb and the " Ball " bombs were now the fashion : the Batty, a light bomb which was fairly safe if properly charged ; the Ball bomb, a round, heavy bomb which was ignited by striking on a bracelet like a safety match, a splendid contrivance so long as it did not rain, as events proved in days to come.

We had throwing competitions, and very soon the men became as keen to win the long distance or the accuracy competition as they were at other games of skill and strength.

## CHAPTER XXV

### GOOD-BYE, GUARDS !

WE were lucky in these days in having
Bethune, a town of considerable size, for
our rest place. The enemy's shells had not
up to this time done any very disastrous
damage, and with its shops and market it
was a great change to the men after coming
out of the line. There was a big theatre
here, which I believe is no longer in use, but
we used to have numerous concerts therein,
and regiments would vie with each other in
trying to put on the best show.

There was also an hotel where you could
get quite a good meal, and a café where
officers adjourned to about 5.30 p.m. for
champagne cocktails ; but best of all, there
were large numbers of comfortable houses
where you could feel civilised, sleep between
sheets, and really pretend that all sorts of
things had never happened. Amongst these
houses was a fine château where an old lady

and her daughters continued to live in spite of frequent bombardments, and the dower-house in the same grounds was much sought after as a battalion head-quarters.

On occasion, this grande dame lent her own dining-room for dinner parties, and here I remember dining with the Irish Guards off beautiful plate and in great luxury provided by the hostess. The Prince of Wales was present; also Sir Charles Munro the Corps commander, and other generals, sitting round a table which was beautifully decorated with flowers, and this within four hours of our coming out of muddy trenches.

Now, however, came a sad time for the Herts, for we learnt that the Guards Division was to be formed, and so we were to leave our comrades with whom we had fought since early in November 1914, and who had given us such a royal welcome and never ceased to make us feel we were of themselves.

General Fielding, the Brigadier, afterwards the distinguished commander of the Guards Division, bade us farewell at Le Quesnoy, and told us things which made us proud, and paid us a tribute that was so sincerely uttered that we knew that we had really reached our aim —" to be regarded as amongst the equals of the best of the British Army."

A farewell dinner was given by the officers of the Grenadiers to the Divisional Staff, and I was honoured by an invitation. These partings are sad, but I told the Grenadiers that I supposed the Herts would now have to try and raise the standard of some other brigade, wherefore I soon found myself being shouted down, so we parted the best of friends before I had read them my complete lecture on how soldiers on active service should comport themselves !

On August 19th the Guards marched away. The route was lined by detachments of all the other battalions in the division, but to the Herts were given the place of honour, and a full company lined the route where General Horne took the salute.

Headed by the brass band of the 2nd Division, down the road they marched, and our lads cheered each battalion as they came along, until the end of the column had gone by and the grandest panorama of humanity had passed before our eyes.

.    .    .    .    .

What would happen to us ? Our fate was soon decreed, and to our joy we were to

stay in the 2nd Division as part of the famous
6th Brigade.  We received a very cordial
welcome from Brigadier-General Daly, who
told us that if we came near our reputation,
he would be more than pleased.

## CHAPTER XXVI

### CRATERLAND

WE soon found ourselves astride the La
Bassée Road, and occupying the trench
round the old mill which we had seen the
French capture months before. This sector,
and those north and south, are the scenes of
great mine fighting; in fact, most of this
front for about a mile is nothing but huge
mine craters.

This broken ground made a great obstacle
for an attacking force, as we were later to
find; and, in addition, some of the craters,
notably Etna and Vesuvius south of the
road, were held on either lip by the opposing
forces.

As the enemy was frequently patrolling
these craters, and our patrols were often
out, some very pretty scraps with bombs
used to take place.

.     .     .     .     .

To command a crater you have to fortify

the near lip before the enemy has succeeded in fortifying his lip, otherwise you cannot live comfortably in occupation; but once you have got a protected loop-hole established which commands the crater, then you ought to be able to shoot any one who tries to fortify opposite. To be quite restful, of course, where you can you capture the whole crater, but this is not always possible in No Man's Land, where the trenches are close.

When we took over the Etna line south of the road, the battalion we relieved had commanded the crater until that morning, when at dawn a German sniper, firing over the top of his lip, succeeded in shooting the sentry through the iron loop-hole. As the sentry was killed, the enemy thus got time to erect a loop-hole and to command the crater, and so it was when we came in.

That night a free exchange of bombs took place, many hundreds being thrown before the fight finished, and both sides were convinced that the crater could not be held.

A few days later I was visiting the left of our line when I was nearly knocked off my feet by a mine explosion quite close, and found myself in a shower bath of earth. On inspection we found that Boche had

" blown " in No Man's Land opposite the battalion just on our left, and as the crater was some way from both lines, neither side tried to occupy. Two days after we left this line a mine was blown under the front trench, and our successors had many casualties.

# CHAPTER XXVII

## MINENWERFERS

ALL along this front we were pestered by German Minenwerfers and other trench mortars. There was one particularly obnoxious visitor, known as Silver King, who flew silently through the air with the appearance of a silver torpedo, and when he exploded great damage resulted and large sections of the trench were blown in; in addition, other large bombs were fired at us continually, and as the explosions were terrific and the ground shook for hundreds of yards, sleep was rendered almost impossible.

As I dislike disturbed nights, I decided to enlist the help of the gunners to strafe these nuisances, and so we put on about a dozen spotters whose sole duty was to mark down from different angles the exact spot from which the smoke was seen by day or the flash by night.

We managed to bring our co-operation

to such a fine art that we had special wires
laid, and the gunners so thoroughly entered
into the sport that they had men standing
by; then, as Minnie opened her lips to fire,
the code word was sent, and before she had
exploded, four field howitzer shells were on
voyage to sit on her. Minnie would therefore explode with her mighty crash, and
within about ten seconds, crash, crash, crash,
crash went the howitzers, exploding their
shells all round her lair. The moral of
the troops rapidly improved, and Minnie
spotting became a joy.

After a day or two of this treatment,
enemy Minnie was silenced, and so great
became the Minnie strafe that tiger-hunting
gunners from strange divisions used to come
to my head-quarters to ask if they might join
in. This was most improper, but most
successful, and the field artillery also co-
operated. What happened we do not know,
but I can guess that either we knocked them
out with direct hits or else the Hun infantry,
who shared our vigorous hate, informed
the Minnie people that if they fired again,
German bayonets would for ever silence
them. Be that as it may, we beat them, and
were no more worried.

Our affection for the gunners now deepened,

and we learnt the art of complete co-operation between the two arms.

A propos of trench mortars, I may mention that one day we were visited by a distinguished company of "Brass Hats," as in these times there were rumours of wars and future attacks, and they had come to spy out the land. I was conducting this distinguished company along a trench when a whistle caused me to look up, and there, in full flight I espied a big bomb coming straight in our direction. I called out! "Bomb over," and began the usual cat dance which decides behind which traverse you are going to shelter, when, to my horror, I saw all my generals and staff prone on the floor, and the bomb racing surely towards us; but by the mercy of Heaven it exploded prematurely in the air, so stretcher bearers were not required, and I breathed again.

The natural inclination when a bomb comes over is to hide like a partridge from a hawk, but before you have lived long in bomb land, you learn to watch him very carefully on tip-toes, and if you know his ways you can invariably dodge him, unless he happens to be Silver King or some other speedy gent of that same breed.

## CHAPTER XXVIII

### THE BLOODY FIELD OF LOOS

ALL is bustle, digging proceeds day and night, and all ranks who are not digging are carrying materials, rations, bombs, and other necessary articles to forward dumps; mothers, grandmothers, and other ladies of weight and dignity are coyly hiding their beauty behind; lighter guns and howitzers are collecting souvenirs for the Germans, and a mighty array of shells is appearing, whilst all men are glad that now at last we have the " stuff " to make a great offensive.

The 2nd Division is on the extreme left of the push, with the 5th Brigade north of the La Bassée Canal at Givenchy, the 6th Brigade at Cuinchy, and the 19th Brigade on the right just south of the La Bassée–Bethune road; on their right again, the remainder of the 1st Corps (Gough's); and on their right again, the 4th Corps (Rawlinson's).

This is the first prolonged bombardment
we have given the Huns, for the simple
reason that this is the first time we have
had the shells; and now for four days and
nights we shell their lines, the villages behind, and the roads by which the food is
conveyed to the enemy trenches. All day
long the field guns, firing low over our
trenches, rake the German wire; and all
night long machine guns crackle as they
sweep it to prevent repair of the gaps.

Our guns are taken from us for the centre
of the push, and new artillery from England
comes to try and learn wire cutting. A
gallant scout of the Herts the night before
the attack went along the whole of the
German wire on our front, and reported
that it was intact, with only one small
gap.

This should have dismayed us, but we
were told that our gas would be so effective
that we would merely walk through the
wire at our leisure.

At 5.40 a.m., on September 25th, we loosed
gas upon the enemy. The wind, which was
favourable in Loos and Vermelles, was,
unhappily, unfavourable—or Hunfavourable
as our men would say—opposite us, and the
result was that the gas of the brigade on

our right drifted down in our direction,
whilst ours blew towards the 5th Brigade;
and although we were equipped with helmets,
all prepared, this event was not conducive
to a good start in the attack. The 6th
Brigade were attacking, with the Kings and
the South Staffords in the front line, the
Herts and 1st Berks in support, and the
1st K.R.R. and 5th Liverpools in reserve;
and at 6.30, as the gas lifted, over went the
leading companies of the attacking battalions,
whilst the supporting battalions were all
moving up to the front system. The 6th
Brigade were never able to penetrate the
wire, and, what is more, the enemy, who were
expecting the attack, opened a murderous
machine gun fire, so much so, that of the
leading company of the Kings in front of
us, only the captain—gallant Goff—reached
the German wire; and on getting there he
turned round to find himself alone, the
remainder of his leading platoon having
been wiped out. He thereupon came back
and, miraculous to narrate, reached our lines
in safety. He was the only officer who had
remained with the 1st Kings from the start,
and later, unhappily, was killed whilst leading his battalion on the Somme.

Meanwhile, the 5th Brigade on our left

had made a considerable advance, although the 19th Brigade on our right had been held up with heavy losses. The remainder of the 1st Corps, however, and the 4th Corps made fine progress, capturing the German front system early in the day, and, later, the whole of the town of Loos and a considerable track of country beyond.

Our attack on the La Bassée Road having failed, we were told for that day to desist from further attempts, whereupon I betook myself to the top of a house at Bradell Point, where, with my telescope, I had a wonderful view of the advance. Quite early I was presented with the magnificent spectacle of a battery of horse artillery galloping forward past the old trenches, and where I was it looked as if the battery could not live, for shells were bursting all round them; but I suddenly saw them swing round and, in spite of riderless horses tearing wildly over the country, in about a minute I saw the flash of each gun, and I knew that the whole battery was in action. Then we could see Infantry going forward in artillery formation, whilst others were digging like fury on the high ground east of Loos, and we saw large numbers of prisoners coming back.

During that night we sent up large parties of men to assist the Kings in bringing in their casualties, and all night long they worked with a will and assisted in bringing in some scores of wounded men.

We of the Herts had been fortunate that day, for in spite of the very heavy barrage as we were reinforcing, we had hardly any casualties to report by evening.

On the 26th we were ordered to relieve the Kings in the front line.

I visited the trenches that night, and all was wonderfully calm in our sector after the fury of the preceding forty-eight hours, but just as I was concluding my round, some silly fellow from the next battalion shouted in a very loud voice, as if he was leading an attack : " Come on, chaps ! " whereupon the Boche properly got the " wind up," thinking that another attack had just started against him, and we cursed our witty friend, finding ourselves for half an hour in a perfect tornado of shells and mortars. The Germans had evidently wired through S.O.S., and were loosing coloured lights into the heavens, with the result that within 100 yards of where I crouched, in one minute there was something like 130 high-explosive shells and mortar bombs bursting. The air was thick with fumes and dust, and the wonderful thing is, that in spite of such volcanic gun and mortar fire, we only had one man buried and one slightly wounded.

The next morning further news came in of the big fight, and we realised that substantial gains had been made by our army and the French, but the British Infantry, which we had seen so gallantly advance as far as the village of Haisnes, had been forced to retire as the troops on their flanks had been held up.

Looking from my observation post I had a wonderful view of the famous slag heap, Fosse 8. In the first attack the British had managed to get round this great coal dump, which was hundreds of yards long, very steep, and with a flat surface at the top, forming a sort of Gibraltar standing up in the middle of otherwise flat country; but, unhappily, they were unable to maintain themselves against very strong counter-attacks. This day, therefore, our troops again attacked, and I could see khaki figures swarming right up the steep banks of the fosse; and then advancing at a double across the flat surface at the top, half the fosse was theirs, when a terrific barrage of enemy artillery opened and the attackers

gradually faded away under a terrible concentrated fire. About an hour later the
scene was reversed, and grey figures swarmed
along that fatal surface. Immediately our
guns came into action and hundreds of the
grey figures were seen to fall, the attack
absolutely withering up under our barrage.
In this last attack the shooting of the
artillery was indeed wonderful, and within
about a minute had turned the fosse into
a cemetery. Our heavies were now pounding the houses south-east of the fosse,
and substantial-looking brick cottages were
lifted bodily into the air from time to time;
but it was evident by now that Loos was
to be no walk-over, and in spite of a large
capture of prisoners, guns, and territory,
it did not look as if there was to be any
piercing of the line on this occasion.

# CHAPTER XXIX

## THE BATTLE OF LOOS CONTINUED

ON our left the 5th Brigade had had to come back, partly because we had failed to advance on their right, and partly because their bomb supply failed at a most important moment. On our immediate right little progress had been made, but farther south terrific fighting still continued, and further efforts were made to win Fosse 8, whilst Hohenzollern Redoubt, the Quarries, and Hill 70 had all had their bloody contests. I am told by onlookers that the advance of the Guards Division against Hill 70 in artillery formation was one of the finest spectacles that soldiers could wish to witness; but although they won the top of the hill it was swept by a terrific barrage, and with terrible gaps in their ranks they were forced to step back over the ridge and dig in just on our side of the crest.

On September 27th a big attack was

planned again against the dump at Fosse 8, and as the wind was in the right direction we were ordered to make another effort at Cuinchy if, after sending out patrols, we found that the gas had been effective.

Final orders were issued in a hurry and had to be wired through to companies, and as I feared there might be some mistake I decided to go up to the line, so that I could personally judge what effect our gas attack was having. The gas was loosed at 5 p.m. and was to run for twenty-five minutes. I had ordered the whole of the attacking companies into dugouts, with orders only to emerge at 5.35, when patrols were to go out. When I arrived in the trenches, therefore, only the gas experts and a few sentries could be seen, and the gas was blowing beautifully over to the enemy's trenches. It was spotted at once, and immediately the Germans put up a big barrage on our trenches, whilst in less than a minute they had lit bonfires on their parapet all the way along their line opposite us.

The scene was weird in the extreme, as dusk was coming on; and whilst the clouds of yellow gas rolled over, hundreds of fires appeared at intervals along the line. These fires, our gas experts tell us, are no use and are merely used by the enemy to give his men confidence. Be that as it may, the gas certainly seemed to lift on reaching the fires, or else the effect on the chemicals was to clarify the gas.

At 5.35 p.m. our patrols went out, and I watched one which went over from where I stood. The patrol consisted of a corporal and two privates, and they had just got through our wire when a machine gun dropped one private with five bullet wounds, and the other private took cover beside his comrade. By this time machine guns were barking in all directions and the corporal walked back to the trenches, climbed over the parapet, and came to his company commander, smacked his rifle very smartly, and reported, " Enemy machine guns active, sir." If one had not realised that this brave fellow had just come from what looked like certain death, it would have been impossible to prevent oneself roaring with laughter at his matter-of-fact voice. Yes, the machine guns were active, and, what is more, directly the patrols went out the enemy lined his parapet in large numbers and our lads opened rapid fire, with the result that many a Boche rolled back ; but the wire was intact and the enemy were unaffected by the gas, and so I ordered the whole of the attackers except snipers and sentries back to their dugouts whilst the enemy barrage continued.

To revert to the patrols. The Germans began to fire on the wounded man lying out, and the earth was flying up round where he lay, so a young sergeant of the Herts ran out to him, lifted him on his back and brought him in, a very gallant act amongst the many courageous deeds of those days.

Nearly all the patrols who went out that evening were wiped out, and it was a fine thing to find men so ready to volunteer to walk in No Man's Land, and so prove whether it was possible for their comrades to advance, when most probably they would pay with their lives in the act of proof.

Once again, considering the terrific bombardment, our losses had been slight; and although we had not been over the top we believe we inflicted thirty or forty casualties, whilst ours could be counted on one hand. This was the more remarkable as the two companies in support had to go up and come back a communication trench which was heavily barraged.

## CHAPTER XXX

### THE BATTLE OF LOOS ENDS

ON September 30th we were relieved by the
9th Cheshires, and as this was the first time
we had been relieved by the New Army we
were very much interested in our relievers,
who proved to be a fine stamp of men.
The relief only started late, and we arrived
back in Bethune in the early hours of the
morning, very much fatigued after a very
prolonged tour in the trenches. For months
the Herts had never been out of the shell
area, and when we were not in the line we
were digging under fire, and this had continued for six weeks on end; and, as a matter
of fact, we had had no rest for more than
one week since December 1914. The longed-
for holiday was not to be yet, and we soon
got orders to move back to the guns, and
this time we were ordered to the centre
of the big battlefield. Marching to Vermelles, which we reached at dusk, we found

the village a still more battered wreck than before, as the Hun gunners had been busy with this little place all through the recent fighting. In the history of this war few spots will be more proudly remembered than Vermelles, for it was here that the French, nine months before, fought their way, yard by yard, and house to house, in a battle which lasted months.

We arrived at Vermelles just before dusk and proceeded along the Hulluch road just as it became dark. Heavy firing could be heard in front, and after we had gone a few hundred yards, bullets began to splash all round us in menacing fashion. So I decided, although the communication trench was a quagmire, that we would use it, and one by one the whole battalion dropped in to the deep trench, whilst the companies in rear lay down flat in the road. We had about a mile to go up that trench, and the going was terrible, as the trench had collapsed in many parts, the telephone wires were a network of obstacles across the track, the footboards were broken where they existed, and the mud was in its most slippery condition. To add to all our troubles our guides had not turned up, but fortunately I had been round the line in daylight, and

I hoped to fetch up right.  We entered the
trench at 7.30 p.m., and not till 1 o'clock
was my last company in position.  Had
we gone on down the road we should have
got to our trench by 8.30; but I had learnt
in this war that the greatest thing is the
preservation of British lives, and this was
emphasised that night, for whereas we had
two casualties, a battalion starting after us,
which took this road, lost thirty-seven,
although they beat us by two hours.

The line we held was a support line immediately in rear of the Quarries, that scene
of violent fighting which was held by the
1st Battalion of the K.R.R., and we actually
held the old British front trenches from
which the attack started.

The trench was littered with equipment
and all the signs of heavy work.

Away on our left the fighting at Hohenzollern Redoubt never seemed to cease, the
bursting of bombs and trench mortars con-
tinuing incessantly.  Once or twice we heard
sharp firing in front, and then star shells
would light the scene; and on one such
occasion I stood up on a fire step to see
what was up, and I found myself looking
into the face of a man a foot away on the
parapet—a dead man.

When dawn came we set to work to clear the battlefield, and collected hundreds of rifles, equipment, etc., and sent them all down to the collecting dump, and the companies got to work in reliefs to repair our trenches, which were much knocked about by artillery fire.

At midday I got a request from the 60th Rifles to lend them a company, as things were hot in front. Our machine guns had already gone up the previous evening.

At night we started to dig new communicating trenches forward to the 60th, so that we could reinforce under cover, and by dawn we had two quite respectable ditches up to them, along which men could march unseen.

We also sent out parties during night to bury all the dead we had marked during the day, and the battlefield soon began to look more normal.

During this day we were shelled, but as we had lots of room, we managed to move the men about directly the shelling began, and thus avoided casualties. On the third day we heard that the Guards Division were coming in to relieve us, and our old friends, the 2nd Grenadiers, were to take over from us, and the 2nd Coldstream to relieve the 60th.

All the afternoon the 60th and our forward company were heavily shelled, and it became clear that Boche was going to counter attack. So we dispatched parties forward with bombs to our comrades in front, and up they went through the barrage with their loads.

About four o'clock the firing became very intense round the Quarries, and our front line was heavily shelled; and just as the Grenadiers came up to relieve us, the line in front became a hell of din and we were reluctant to depart whilst our No. 1 Company was " sticking it " out there.

As we marched off our guns started an intense fire, and we knew that an attack was taking place, so when we arrived at the Brigade Head-quarters dug-out, the regiment lay down whilst I went in to ask the Brigadier if we were wanted before marching off. Just at that moment a messenger arrived at the brigade office with a most urgent message for bombs and bombers, and the Brigadier asked us to help. Our men were very tired, and I went out to them as they lay resting on the side of a trench and called for volunteers to go down to Vermelles and carry up bombs. In a minute a hundred tired men, who knew they had a long march before them, were off at a double for Vermelles, and very soon the Herts bombers and carrying parties were once again winding up the long trench with their heavy burdens.

When they arrived the 60th were at the end of their bomb supply, and very grateful they were for our reinforcement.

We then learnt that the 60th had indeed had a warm time. During that day two Herts machine guns had been buried, and in one case with all the team knocked out, save one; the sole survivor had dug his gun and ammunition out and had mounted his gun again just in time to open fire on a stream of Germans rushing up a shallow communication trench to the attack. For hours a bomb fight had been joined, but every attack of the enemy was beaten back, and eventually the Coldstream took over and the last of the Herts were on the march back to Bethune, where, thoroughly exhausted, they arrived in the early hours of the morning.

# CHAPTER XXXI

## FAREWELL TO THE HERTS

THIS time we really did get some rest, and the Battle of Loos, as far as the British were concerned, was over.

On October 8th we were holding a big concert in the theatre when distant firing assumed an ominous tone, and a messenger rushed into the theatre to say the 5th and 6th Brigades will return at once to billets. I sent out messengers all over Bethune, and then we got our orders to move. Within half an hour of the receipt of the order all rations were served out and water bottles full, and we paraded in the dark in the Grande Place, with only two men absent, and marched off with much singing back towards the line.

We bivouacked at Beuvry and waited for orders and news. Something was happening, and we realised that the Germans were making a big counter-attack.

We soon had our bivouac fixed, and then the men sang songs round camp fires, whilst the other battalions of the brigade came marching up in the dark to the rendezvous.

Cookers were ordered up, and a hot meal was just finished, and we were ready for anything when news came through that the enemy had made a great effort to regain his lost ground, but that all his efforts had withered up in front of the British line, and that he had bumped especially into the Guards Division with great disaster. The Guards had had a good shoot, and so had the neighbouring divisions, and the official news next day was to the effect that the German attack had failed completely, with a loss of 8,000 casualties. This was the last and greatest effort of the Germans to win back the victory of Loos. This offensive had proved that, given sufficient munitions, the German line can be stormed, but that the limited objective is at present the wise course and that the problem of strong posts is still unsolved, unless each objective can be hammered in turn. Loos, with all its losses, has however given us a feeling of moral superiority over the Boche, and perhaps the Loos salient may some day be of

value when we cross the Vimy Ridge to the
south.

.    .    .    .    .

Now began a tedious winter, with many
tours in the trenches between Loos and
Festubert, in which we had to sit still under
many bombardments and, as Christmas approached, had to contend with much water,
so much so that at Festubert we had to
content ourselves with holding islands; and
all the breastworks we had built with such
great care gradually collapsed under our
eyes, and all we could do was to repeatedly
rebuild our islands.

.    .    .    .    .

Two battalions of the New Army came
into our brigade and two of the old regular
battalions departed.    One of the new battalions was attached to us for instruction,
the 13th Essex, and great friends we became.
Months afterwards this battalion greatly
distinguished itself on the Somme.

.    .    .    .    .

Another time the Footballers' Battalion
of the Royal Fusiliers sent companies to
us in the trenches for instruction, and I
remember one company came up into the
line just as a very heavy shelling was taking
place—a trying moment for new hands.

I was leading the company into the front line when I suddenly heard one of the Footballers blow a shrill blast on his whistle. I turned round and asked what the devil he was doing, and he replied, " Well, sir, I thought it was just about 'arf time."

.    .    .    .    .

Christmas comes, and this time we have a great officers' banquet at the La France Hotel, and much feasting amongst all ranks, football, drill, and high spirits. The winter drags out its weary course and the army is gradually growing in numbers and guns, and next time we shall see.

.    .    .    .    ,

On February 6th I received orders to take command of a Brigade.

I was naturally pleased at promotion, but it is with a heavy heart that you leave men with whom you have lived in the palace of death for sixteen months, and my feelings were the more sad because my lads had shown those qualities of loyalty and devotion to duty which makes one feel that they are friends who make campaigning a joy.

The "Herts Guards" won great favour in all the area of the Bethune district, and wherever we went the inhabitants would turn out to show how glad they were to see

us again, and never once did I have a serious
complaint of their conduct from civilians.
Crime was practically non-existent and sickness slight.

A curious fact with regard to sickness
was, that whenever we were due for the
trenches, no one reported sick, and apparently it was considered in the ranks bad
form to go sick if there was any danger
about. These are the little things which
make one so proud of the British soldiers in
France, for it proves that in spite of " grous-
ing," " swearing," and other little vices,
there is nobility there, which proves that,
given the chance, our race still possesses
all that goes to make men great.

So on a February morning I said good-
bye to the Herts, and saw them march by
for the last time. I conjured up recollec-
tions of the days when these fine men, as
boys, used to march up to the park at home
for little field days; how we went together
to the range and to camp; and how the old
volunteers became the Territorials. I had
seen them grow up, and for years we had
played at soldiers together, and then, when
the great adventure called, the Herts had
responded, and—God bless them !—they have
been through a thousand hells and have

ever remained soldiers and gentlemen.
They had not been found wanting.

.        .        .        .

*Note.*—The Herts, months after I left
them, were in the attack at Thiepval, at
Swaben, and in the big attack in the Ancre,
where, advancing for 1,600 yards in perfect
order, they captured their objective in
masterly form, took some 300 prisoners,
consolidated and repelled counter-attacks,
and marched back with a minimum number
of casualties.

Again, in July 1917, the Herts advanced
in magnificent style, but on reaching their
objective found themselves "in the air,"
with unbroken wire in front of them. They
were attacked on three sides and a desperate
fight ensued. Every single officer was either
killed or wounded, but the Herts fought on
first under the sergeant-major, then when
he fell under a sergeant, and finally the
remnants retired fighting doggedly under
the chaplain, and dug in. In this action
Colonel Page, the gallant commander, was
killed whilst organising a counter-attack.

# PART II
# THE NEW ARMY

# CHAPTER I

## THE NEW ARMY

On February 8th, 1916, I sped northwards, in a motor and came to Erquinghem, near Armentières, to take over the command of the 🔲 Infantry Brigade on the very 23 Divi: night that the brigade was going up to the trenches. Armentières, which is just behind the British line, was interesting to me, as one of my forbears was governor of that city some centuries before the *entente cordiale*. It is with an odd feeling that one enters new surroundings in a new country and finds oneself amongst strangers, and I must confess to the sensation of a new boy at school when I arrived at my headquarters.

My embarrassment was not lessened when I found that all my battalion commanders were men of previous war experience and very much my senior in age, but I soon found that they were determined to make my task easy; and in spite of the fact that

I was a Territorial and they all regulars, I
realised that I was dealing with men to
whom the war came first, with personal
considerations buried a long way behind.

When the history of the New Army comes
to be written, no mean tribute should be
paid to the ex-regulars who, in many cases,
had to build up and instruct the new units
practically single-handed, as frequently they
had no one of any previous military knowledge to assist them.   On those men—who
had in some cases left active life behind,
and who again got into harness and, after
most exacting preparation, led their battalions to France with all the discomforts of
trench life, all the nerve-racking din of
modern war and all the responsibility of
leading raw troops—the strain must have
been great, and all honour is due to these
fine English gentlemen for the great part
they played.

    .          .          .          .

The 68th Brigade Infantry consisted of four
battalions of the New Army, two battalions
of the Northumberland Fusiliers and two of
the Durham Light Infantry.   No battalion
had more than two officers with previous
military service, and none were on the
active list at the outbreak of war.

10 NF, 11 NF
12 DLI, 13 DLI

The non-commissioned officers were equally inexperienced, very few having seen any kind of military service prior to the war.

The men were fine, big fellows, many of whom were miners, a likely lot to do credit to the bayonet when opportunity offered.

.   .   .   .   .

My head-quarters were in a farm which was also occupied by its owners, for here the cultivation of the soil went on well forward of Brigade Head-quarters.

To reach the line we usually rode to a shattered village which was frequently shelled, and went thence by communication trenches to the front system, which at this time of the year was in a poor state owing to the weather. Only breast-works were possible, owing to the watery state of the soil and the fact that we were on a level with the river Lys and its several small tributaries which run by and through the trenches. The result of this watery ground was, that great sections of breast-work were continually falling in, and the troops led a very muddy and uninteresting existence, with occasional patrol encounters in No Man's Land, which was wider in these parts than I had yet experienced. When after about fifteen days we had orders to

the effect that the division was to be relieved,
I was not sorry, for six months in this part
of the world, with no chance of training,
was hardly conducive to improvement, and
all ranks were " fed up " with this dull flat
land.

.        .        .        .        .

We guessed we should go south, and we
guessed right; but first we marched to the
Hazebrucke neighbourhood, which I had
not visited since November 1914, and we
marched thither on a very frosty morning
along very slippery roads.

We discovered that our mobility was not
quite perfect, and winged words flew around;
but we knew that our stationary life was
chiefly responsible, and we determined to
improve.

After a day or two's rest, the brigade
entrained for Bruay area, and was billeted
in Marles-les-Mines and district. Here we
spent a few days getting fit and drilling,
and our miners made friendly invasions
against the French mines, and many of our
men were not satisfied until they had had
a shift in the pits. We now heard that
our division was to be attached to another
corps, and we moved up to billets in Fresni-
court district.

This country of Artois is a jolly change after Flanders, as there are hills and woods and comfortable quarters, with many commodious châteaux and capital huts for the men.

# CHAPTER II

## SOUCHEZ

THE division was now ordered to take over from the French the line in front of Souchez village, with one brigade in the line, one in support, and our own in reserve. This was to me by far the most fascinating spot I had yet visited, and I spent many hours examining the immortal battlefield where France won back the great spur of Notre Dame de Lorette and fought and won her bloody hand-to-hand fights in Souchez and Carency, with the culminating blow which secured the slopes of Vimy Ridge and almost won the ridge itself.

No soldiers could want a more interesting ramble than round this historic field, the only drawback being that Vimy Ridge frowns down on you from its great brown mass, and if you linger too long on the road Boche snipes at you with field guns, which is an attention far too personal to be appreciated.

As you approach Ablain St. Nazaire village, Notre Dame leaves its sloping green surface and becomes more precipitous and rocky, great ravines run into the southern face, from which ideal artillery positions French guns were noisily and with many an echo rolling up the hill pouring their wrath upon the enemy. Here the guns were ensconced behind an almost sheer wall of hillside, and nothing apparently except an enemy howitzer could stop them at their business. Ablain village is a scarred and battered place, and there the underground life is the mode, for if any group of men or any vehicle honoured the street, then a bouquet of shrapnel would send you running for dear life. So the transport only creeps up after dark, and the individual by day is not wont to linger.

Here I entered what I believed was my future head-quarters—a week afterwards it was vacated as dangerous—and then I passed on down the village and saw the remains of the church, just one face of the tower still standing silhouetted against Notre Dame, which made an imposing background; and there one sees the great strength of the spur itself rising almost sheer up out of Souchez valley, and we could almost

13

picture the blue Poilu as he hunted the grey
Boche down the side of that cliff.

We then come to the sugar factory, levelled
to the ground by months of shelling, a piece
of twisted machinery surrounded by bricks
marking the place where the *sucrerie* had
been, around which hundreds died in some
of the fiercest fighting of the war. Close
by is the cemetery, where the hallowed
ground was churned up to such an extent
that the dead, ancient and modern, lay
side by side, and perhaps the spirits of the
heroes of Condé's great fights stretched a
hand to France's newest dead and hailed
them worthy of the soil.

Carency, once a village, now only a
glorious name, lies beside the Souchez river,
where the guns of France had to blast their
way and where, ever since, the German
gunners had spat out their wrath.

Prior to Verdun, with the possible exception of Ypres, no country had claimed such
a toll of dead as this, and even when we
arrived there were many signs of this year-
old death grip.

On the top of Notre Dame there lay a
German, and prone across him a Frenchman. Each had given and each received the
*coup de grâce*. Surely the withered remains,

which still lay there on the crest of the hill at the time I speak of, were a symbol of that great conflict, and perhaps a little more; for although both died, the Frenchman was on top—and then the British came.

# CHAPTER III

## CALONNE

THE snow had cleared away and the weather began to improve when we heard of a change of plan and moved north of the Notre Dame Ridge, with orders for the division to take over the three-brigade front from the Souchez river to the railway north of Calonne.

To the —— Brigade was allotted the Calonne sector, where we relieved old comrades of mine.

Calonne itself is a mining village which is situated right on the line of trenches, the eastern face of the village actually forming part of the front line, whilst, almost opposite Calonne, is the Cité de Corneilles on the German front system. This was a most interesting sector and very strongly fortified. One feature of the front trench was peculiar, because the line ran over a big slag heap which was always on fire, and had been so for, I believe, some fifty years, and whenever the enemy shelled the heap it was inclined to burst into flames. The trench was not pleasant in Calonne village, because, when the enemy shelled, many bricks flew around, and if a piece of shell missed you, you always had a chance of a brickbat.

The line, which had recently been taken over from the French, required a good deal of work, but the communication trenches in Calonne were remarkably well built and revetted with pit props.

From Calonne back to Bully Grenay, there was no covered way, and the road was overlooked by the enemy, which made it very unpleasant by day when it was shelled, and more so by night as bullets were numerous; so much so, that we had a few casualties on the way up to relieve on the first night.

So I made up my mind to spend the first part of our time in making our defences strong and providing a good communication trench, and the whole brigade put its back into the work of improving the line.

After a short time we got the front line perfect and the support line fair; and, simultaneously, the two resting battalions dug two magnificent communication trenches.

My head-quarters at the start were in

Calonne village, but as two enemy high explosives penetrated the upper storey one night whilst I was at dinner, my Divisional General told me to establish new quarters at Bully Grenay, where we were most comfortable, in spite of occasional shelling.

Calonne had now become so strong and its communications so good, that I decided to encourage offensive tactics, and this seemed the more desirable as our comrades on our right had very poor trenches, whereas we had good shelters and cellars, and it was therefore expedient from every point of view to draw fire and waste enemy ammunition, especially as our position was so strong that we rather invited hostilities in any form.

Night after night, therefore, we sallied forth with small fighting patrols in No Man's Land, which succeeded in running into several Boche working parties and inflicting many casualties, whilst all day our snipers kept adding to our bag.

I was very proud of my sector, and we had numerous visitors. One day, the Corps Commander, Sir Henry Wilson, desired to see our reserve line, so I conducted him down our new-made communication trench, when, to my annoyance, the enemy began shelling the trench, just by what is known as Condé's tree, near a monument to the same celebrity.  I accordingly, thinking myself very wise, suggested to my distinguished visitor that we should take a circuitous route round some old trenches.  As bad luck would have it, the German shells pursued us away to the flank.  At last, feeling rather hot, we arrived in the reserve line, and here I thought by doubling to the right again we should surely avoid our persecutors. Not a bit of it; German shrapnel kept on bursting within twenty yards of us, or less, and I bethought me of a gunners' observation post where there was a shallow dugout, and down the steps of this haven we jumped, only to get a couple of direct hits on the dugout itself.  In a minute or two we decided to push on, and only reached peaceful surroundings when we got to Calonne village. Here I assured the Corps Commander everything would be quiet, and I was just describing the virtues of the village line when the enemy again commenced firing, and so we again beat a retreat towards home.  What the Corps Commander thought of his " happy Sunday afternoon " with me I do not know, but as he cracked jokes the whole time, I hope he enjoyed it.

A day or two afterwards, Sir Hubert Gough, the Corps Commander immediately on my left, desired a guide to see where we joined up, and I sallied forth with him and a goodly company of Staff officers. We came to the railway on the left of the Calonne sector, and the general expressed a desire to see a machine gun emplacement which swept the railway towards the enemy. I expostulated, as it was a very bright day, but a Staff officer of the next division thought it was safe, so down the railway the general and a Staff officer went, and I followed a hundred yards behind, so as not to form too noticeable a group, and the remainder of the party waited for us to return. The Huns saw us and opened fire with field guns just as the Corps Commander reached the machine gun dugout, and in he tumbled; but I was not so lucky, as I had no hole—only the bare bank of the embankment, on which I spreadeagled whilst half a dozen shrapnel burst along the railway, missing me by a very few yards.

I remained in my uncomfortable position until the famous general came running back, doing a half-mile in good time, and then I followed, with a record sprint.

My Cook's Tours with Corps Com-

manders were getting rather too warm to
be amusing.

. . . . .

Now I was anxious to kill Boches opposite
Calonne, and the corps was anxious to strafe
the famous Pimple on Vimy Ridge; and as
it was undesirable that the enemy should
" counter strafe " our poor trenches at
Souchez, the two schemes appeared to offer
good co-operative results. My plan was to
make the enemy think we were going to
attack him and get him to man his trenches
and bring up supports, and then give him a
really heavy bombardment whilst we were
safely stowed away in dugouts and cellars.
To excite the enemy and to add to the illusion,
we dug assembly trenches two days before,
and made considerable preparations, cutting
wire with artillery, and by night raking the
gaps with machine guns; and on the morning
of April 10th we made a great display of
scaling ladders in the reserve line, and half
a dozen heroes, with fixed bayonets, kept
on marching round this line and successfully
drew fire.

At 1.30 we began to bombard the enemy,
and showed more bayonets in the reserve
line. Our bombardment was quite considerable, and whilst our field howitzers

were playing havoc with the houses in the
Cité de Corneilles, a 9-inch howitzer pumped
sixty rounds at a great pit head which overlooked our line, causing great delight to all
beholders. At about four o'clock we gave
an intense bombardment of all guns, mortars,
and about 200 rifle grenades, and then suddenly we let loose sham gas, which blew
over to the enemy's trenches, and all guns
lifted. Now we could hear the Germans
shouting " Gaz " and beating gongs for dear
life, and at a given signal, all our guns came
down again on the German trenches, and
all our mortars and rifle grenadiers opened
a few rounds and then took cover.

There is no doubt that we thoroughly
deceived the enemy, who must have been
thick in his trenches when our guns shortened
and all our missiles hurtled at him whilst
the smoke blew over, and as a result, he
put up a very big barrage between our front
and support trenches where none of our
men were, and where none intended to go,
because we were all, like " brer Fox," lying
very low and thoroughly enjoying the noise.

The enemy was seen to line his parapet,
and our snipers had the time of their lives,
and at a conservative estimate we are sure
that we inflicted in these operations thirty

visible casualties, apart from what our guns
may have done.  Our total casualties were
one officer and six other ranks, and the
enemy wasted nearly 2,000 rounds of shell
on us whilst we were under cover.  The
result of this operation was, that all ranks,
both infantry and gunners, felt that we had
thoroughly punished the enemy.

.          .          .          .          .

After these episodes the " stuff " began
to fly a bit, and Calonne lost some of its
houses, but we kept up our offensive tactics,
and the Durhams on the left got home one
night with great effect by a bomb attack
on a working party, whilst the Northumber-
lands on the right also created a diversion
which unhappily did not come off.

Here there were two saps, very close
together, being only about twenty yards
apart, with very thick wire in between;  and
as our sap was in hand-bombing distance of
the enemy, we decided to make an effort to
destroy the enemy's sap.  In order to do
this and clear away the huge mass of wire
entanglement, we determined to try and
blow the wire up with an explosive torpedo.
We secured a torpedo, and two very gallant
men from the Northumberland Fusiliers
crawled out at night with the six-foot tor-

pedo and succeeded in placing it under the German wire and lighting the fuse, when they hurriedly retired. Unhappily, however, something was amiss with the torpedo, and it did not go off, and the same men crawled out again and brought the torpedo back, very angry at having run such risks for nothing.

At this same spot a most unfortunate incident occurred. The Adjutant of the Northumberland Fusiliers, Captain the Hon. J. G. Joicey, an extremely gallant officer, went out to examine the wire, and was unfortunately killed by a bomb between the two saps. Several efforts were made the same night, under heavy fire, to recover his body, and a gallant volunteer actually crawled out and tied a wire round the body; but when our men in the sap began to pull on the wire, it unhappily snapped.

Now we were afraid that possibly Captain Joicey had maps or information on him when killed, and so we decided the next night to make a big effort to try and bring him in, and our plan was to open intense artillery and mortar fire on the German sap and then to rush out and bring him in. Unhappily, the enemy conceived the same idea, and a quarter of an hour before our bombardment was to commence, they opened a terrific fire and secured the body in the confusion.

After about a fortnight we were relieved in the Calonne sector by another brigade, and went back to rest.

## CHAPTER IV

### SOUCHEZ AGAIN

AFTER leaving the Calonne sector the brigade went out to the rest area, where for the first time since it arrived in France we were able to undergo serious training. We were quartered in various villages near the river Lys, and practised open warfare, and a very marked improvement in discipline, drill, marching, and field work was soon evident.

After a happy and strenuous time we marched back by easy stages to the Bruay district, and from thence, after a few days as brigade in reserve, we went into the line immediately north of the Souchez river and relieved the 24th Brigade.

This sector was in very poor condition, the front trenches being constantly blown in by trench mortar and shell fire on the left, whilst the right was absolutely dominated by the enemy on Vimy Ridge, which

looked straight down on our system. The
enemy snipers were very active here, and
a few men got shot in the head the first forty-
eight hours in, so I determined to deepen
the whole of the right and to make a complete new support line and communication
trenches. We had a prolonged stay in this
line, and the conditions got more lively as
the time went on; but thanks to the good
weather and hard work, before we handed
over to our successors we had a fair front
line, a perfect support line, and a good
reserve line in the front system.

The trench was on the lower slope of the
spur, and here, as in the front system, digging
was difficult owing to the large number of
graves of French and German dead—killed
in the great fighting of a year before.

I mentioned in a previous chapter that
the trenches on the Vimy slopes south of the
Souchez river were very poor, and this fact
the enemy who dominated them also apparently realised, for after a terrific bombardment he made a big attack on the division
on our right and their neighbours. The
London Territorials' trenches were almost
completely destroyed, and when the German avalanche rushed down the hill upon
them, their front line did not give, but

died gamely, and so the gallant little Cockneys were overwhelmed and the Germans advanced farther down the slopes of Vimy.

I watched this attack with considerable anxiety from Notre Dame. The din was hideous, and I could see the star shells ever coming closer on my right. It transpired that the Germans had advanced 800 to 1,000 yards, and if they had come another 1,000 yards we should have been involved, but the attack was now held.

A night attack on Vimy, viewed from Notre Dame, was a wonderful spectacle. The firework display, looking up on the height, was wonderful, as lights and rockets went up in scores, and the flashes of thousands of bursting shells added to the extraordinary effect, whilst the echo of the guns and shell bursts along the Souchez valley were weird in the extreme.

.        .        .        .        .

About this time I organised a raid for June 2nd, which was duly carried out by the Durham Light Infantry. I favoured a small raid, and twenty-five picked officers and men were told off for the work. Twice during the day the group of artillery covering us gave an intense bombardment, whilst our mortars cut a gap in the wire, and the idea was, for the infantry to leave our trenches whilst our field artillery was actually firing on the enemy trench and whilst our mortars were firing over the heads of the infantry.

When I state that the trenches at the point selected were just under seventy yards apart, it will be realised that we had some confidence in our artillery.

Punctual to the moment, as our artillery commenced one minute's intense bombardment, the raiders left our trench and were crossing our wire whilst our shells were bursting on the German trench. Precisely at the minute's conclusion, the guns on the objective ceased, and those to either flank continued. Our raiders entered the German trench without casualty, and separated according to plan. Breathless moments these for the raiding party. The officer leading ran straight into two Huns and shot them both; they continued along the pitch-dark trench when they came to a sap. The second officer, turning down here, suddenly sees a German; he snaps at him with an automatic pistol which misfires, the German fires his rifle and misses at two yards and charges with his bayonet; again the automatic pistol

14

fails to fire, when, by the greatest luck, the
first officer, hearing the noise, rushes up and
there, in the narrow sap, shoots the German
dead over the shoulder of his friend.

A Durham in the main trench is now
engaged in a life-and-death bayonet fight
with a huge German. The officer dare not
fire his revolver, because parry and thrust,
advance and retreat go on between these
two, and to shoot might be fatal to the
wrong man; but the Durham lad was no
chicken, and after as pretty a bout as can
be desired, he killed his man.

Meanwhile, a sergeant, leading the party
which turns right, bayonets three Germans
in quick succession, and the bombing party
is at work. Five great dugouts, lit by elec-
tricity and teeming with Germans, are duly
bombed, and death is dealt with a free hand.

I had given implicit orders that I must
have a live German for identification purposes, and a small Durham was accordingly
marching off a huge Hun when suddenly, in
the pitch-dark, the German realises he is
near the entrance to a dugout which was
unknown to our man, so he hurls himself
down the dugout entrance, lugging the escort
with him. Just as the Durham is disap-
pearing down the hole, one of his comrades

arrives on the scene and, by slinging his
bayonet down the hole, kills the big man
just in time, and so perishes my live Hun.

Now the whistle blows and the raiders
retire through the gap in the wire, which
had been cut by a special party detailed,
and a rocket goes up, and guns, mortars, and
grenades all pour in their fire to cover the
retirement of the raiders, whilst Lewis and
machine guns rake the enemy trench right
and left, and behold, the whole of the raiders
are back safe, and one may be excused a
sigh of relief. In this raid, where fighting
in the trench was carried on hand to hand,
the Durhams slew, with bayonet and bullet,
twelve Germans; and at the lowest estimate,
killed twelve Germans in each of the five dugouts bombed, or seventy-two Germans killed.

Our total casualties were two men very
slightly wounded by the back splash of their
own bombs.

The whole operation took three minutes;
a fairly intense three minutes this, and fine
work; but we knew that we owed much to
the perfect shooting of the guns and mortars,
for a single error of a few yards by a gun
might have spoilt the whole show.

.        .        .        .        .

Our raid enraged the Boche, and life became unhealthy in these parts from now onwards. My head-quarters were in a little farmhouse, and the village came in for a tremendous shelling, and we had some lively times.

One day, while we were sitting in our mess room with the signalling officer at the table, a terrific crash occurred, and a time-fuse whistled past my leg, which it obligingly missed by inches, and we dis-covered that the two adjoining bedrooms, happily unoccupied, as the brigade-major and orderly officer were out, were demolished by a 5·9 high explosive.

This kind of thing makes one rather nippy, and next day, when a high explosive burst in the farmyard twenty yards away, I " got the wind up " and yelled " to dugouts." We all cleared, and had just got round the wall of the house when the next shell demolished the mess room where we had all been sitting fifteen seconds before—which only proves that it is well to be active in such times.

Meanwhile, our village was becoming more and more dusty and noisy ; houses were knocked down right and left, and the last of the inhabitants were prevailed upon to leave.

One night a party of marines from the Naval Brigade were marching up to dig, and as I watched them go by, a shell pitched in the midst of one group and three were killed and two wounded.

The enemy bombardment against our trenches was particularly violent, and the point from which we raided was daily destroyed by mortars.

. . . . .

A newly arrived division now sent up companies for instruction, and I was rather amused, going round the line at night, to hear very disparaging remarks concerning our trenches as compared to those at Gallipoli. "This, sir, is child's play," I was told, "compared to that."

The next night, after their trenches had been half levelled, I asked them how the child's play was getting on, and they frankly confessed a desire for the quiet life of Suvla Bay.

. . . . .

We were determined not to be cowed by the enemy's frightfulness, and gave them three mortars for every one they fired at us, and by very gallant work on the part of our mortar teams we almost silenced the enemy's mortars after a few days.

We also decided to raid one of his saps on the right, and twelve men of the Northumberland Fusiliers, under an officer, on June 8th, discovering that the sap was heavily held, made a converging attack from two flanks. When within about twelve yards of the sap, unhappily one of the attackers fell over the trip wire on a steel plate, whereupon the enemy opened fire. The attacking party, therefore, heavily bombed the sap and retired according to orders. As the sap was at the time crowded with Germans, we had good reason to believe that many casualties were inflicted by our bombers, whilst ours were nil.

# CHAPTER V

## TO THE SOMME

THE division was now relieved, and another
division took over our sector whilst we
marched back by easy stages to the training
area. Our first stop was in a very charming
little village where British troops had not
previously been billeted. I was riding on
to the château with my Staff, a little ahead
of the brigade, when I noticed a great deal
of excitement amongst the inhabitants,
who were running in all directions, with
turkeys, geese, and fowls of lesser dignity
under their arms. When I inquired from
my officer interpreter, a gallant Frenchman,
the reason for this agitation, he informed
me that the inhabitants were convinced that
we would clear the place of every kind of
animal, and that therefore all the live stock
was being conveyed to cellars, etc. I had
my little joke at their expense, and desired
him to convey to the citizens that British

soldiers were not living on the country, and that I guaranteed the lives of their birds, whereupon, with much cackling, our feathered friends were allowed to resume their normal existence and the inhabitants proceeded to offer them for sale at outrageous prices, and that night we ate an enormous goose in our mess—the goose was paid for.

The château in which I was billeted was an old house, the property of a French marquise whose ancestors looked down upon us from the walls as we dined. I cannot help thinking that these said ancestors were almost as confused as the inhabitants, especially so when I discovered that our horses were tied up to the identical iron rings which were placed there by British cavalry 100 years ago in the days when the British and French were not allies.

. . . . .

We again found ourselves in the training area, where we had progressive training, ending up in divisional field days, and all ranks of the division greatly improved, when the usual joke went round that we were being " fed up for slaughter "; and then came the great day when we were en-trained for the Somme, towards the end of July.

We detrained at Amiens, where all was bustle, and the crowded city was much interested at our arrival. Amiens was like nothing we had yet seen in France—civil life continued, all the shops were doing a roaring trade, and all sorts of vegetables and fruit found its way into our various messes.

My head-quarters were established in a delightful little château within 300 yards of the Somme, and here we watched troop trains coming up at intervals of every five minutes. And now the great bombardment for the July offensive commenced, and the distant sky at night was lit by a thousand flashes.

Brigadiers were ordered to go up and re-connoitre all the approaches to the British lines, and we spent a very instructive day, motoring all along immediately behind our line and watching the tremendous bombardment of the British guns. Our artillery superiority and our ascendancy in the air were very noticeable, and at the commencement the duel appeared to be very one-sided.

The nature of the country, with its rolling downs, lent itself very well to observation, and after a very noisy but intensely interest-

ing day we motored back to our commands;
and now, each day, we marched forward by
easy stages and bivouacked at Millencourt,
just in rear of Albert, when the great attack
commenced.

# CHAPTER VI

## THE BATTLE OF THE SOMME

ON July 3rd the brigade moved up to Albert, where we lay in trenches for one night. The weather, which was happily fine at the commencement of the operations, continued to be so, and we did not suffer any discomfort from our night out.

The whole of the organisation behind the lines was most interesting, and showed a marked improvement on anything we had yet experienced; and indeed all things looked like business.

In folds of the ground west of Albert there were long lines of guns and howitzers of such calibre that if any one of them had arrived in France in 1914 the whole Army would have wanted to visit so unusual a monster and been overjoyed at its arrival, and as we marched by this formidable line and saw each gun or howitzer jump and make its bow to the enemy, and the teams

204 THE BATTLE OF THE SOMME [PT. II

sweating as they hauled fresh shells into position, we felt much exhilarated.

From Albert we marched on July 4th to Becourt Wood, where the brigade bivouacked. Here the din was so incessant that it was impossible to sleep, and by way of adding to our discomfort rain began to fall and the wood was shelled by enemy field guns.

By this time, of course, the British Army had captured the whole of the first system of trenches on our front, and our division came up in time for the second series of operations, and was allocated the objective, Contalmaison village, to a point just west of Bailiff Wood, both inclusive, and I was informed that one brigade would be responsible for the objective from the western point of Contalmaison village across the valley running thence to Bailiff Wood, the wood itself, and thence to Point 81 on the high ground crossing the western slope of the valley.

Before we could attack this ultimate objective the division would have to capture some intermediate trenches, and I sallied forth with my brigade-major to reconnoitre as far as the enemy permitted.

We were glad to get away from the everlasting din of Becourt Wood and made our way towards the original British line. Here

we saw the first signs of the great battle,
as dead horses lay in pathetic attitudes where
a battery had been rushed up to support the
attack. Passing on, we crossed the old

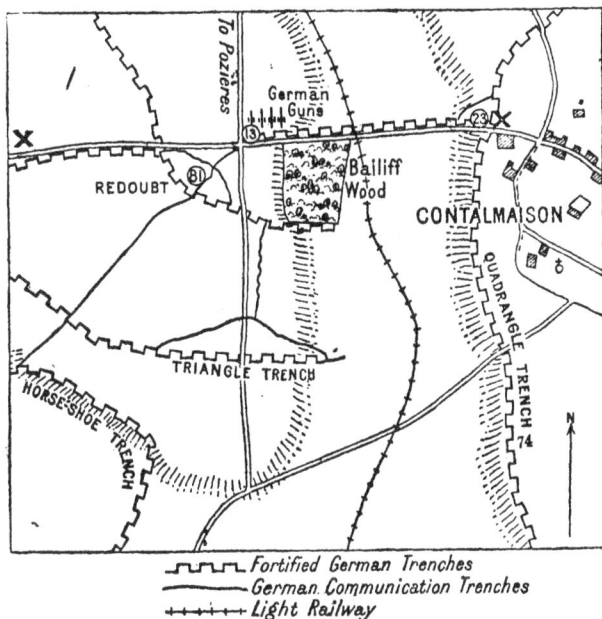

PLAN SHOWING THE JOINT ATTACKS BY THE BRIGADE
ON THE SOMME.

British line and walked over what had been
No Man's Land, that wonderful continuous
racecourse where a hundred thousand British
soldiers had charged with light heart through
a rain of lead only three days before.

Here losses had not been very heavy, and just where we passed not many British dead were visible, but burial parties were out, and soon the battlefield would show little sign of that wonderful rush which heralded the great July. We now reached the old German first line and saw the extraordinary havoc our guns had wrought. The wire was smashed and buried in a thousand craters, and the trench itself was for every few yards obliterated or choked with earth.

As German shells were now falling with some persistence we decided to use what cover the old German trenches afforded, and we saw many a ghastly spectacle : occasional khaki figures lay prone in the trench, and then perhaps a group of dead in grey almost blocking our passage. Sometimes we got out of the trench to avoid these sights, but safety demanded our return to cover, and we were very much relieved when we found ourselves on a sunk road by Lozenge Wood, which was being heavily shelled at that moment, so we edged off westward, and there got a distant view of Contalmaison village and the tops of the trees at Bailiff Wood, returning again over the stricken field to Becourt.

# CHAPTER VII

## ATTACK ON BAILIFF WOOD

ON July 5th we got the splendid news
that a brigade of our division, at a second
attempt, had captured Horseshoe Trench,
and received our orders to attack the main
objective on July 7th as part of a big attack
by large forces on each of our flanks. We
therefore relieved the brigade in Horseshoe
Trench, and I gave orders to the leading
battalion to capture and consolidate a
trench known as the Triangle that night.
This operation was successfully carried out
by the D.L.I. after dark without opposition.

The big attack was due to start at 8 a.m.
on July 7th, but as a brigade of our division
had the difficult task of capturing the
whole length of the village, I got instructions that I was to wait until they were
level with me before starting. As therefore
the heavy artillery was ordered to fire on
Bailiff Wood until 9.30 a.m. I gave orders

to the attacking battalion, the Northumberland Fusiliers, not to assault until 9.15 a.m.

I heard that the next brigade were well under way and had reached the southernmost house of Contalmaison, so at 9.15 the Fusiliers went over the top.

The Germans had turned their barrage on to the valley, and it was by now a cauldron of bursting explosions.

Notwithstanding these conditions the battalion advanced with perfect order, marching in quick step right through the barrage, where things looked about as ugly as possible. On they pressed until they reached a point only fifty yards south of Bailiff Wood; but here our attacking waves came under a terrible enfilade machine gun fire from the trench running along the west of Contalmaison and also a frontal fire from Bailiff Wood and beyond. As our line of advance was entirely dominated from both flanks there was no question of digging in in the valley, as the men were being shot as they lay in the open, so I decided not to throw fresh troops in, and the centre of the Northumberland Fusiliers withdrew after three companies had made a fine effort.

A platoon of the Fusiliers, working on

the right, had captured a small German work, disposing of its garrison and taking twenty-seven unwounded prisoners, and this trench we continued to hold. Another platoon, working on the left, succeeded in digging in under fire on the high ground, and were able to consolidate, thus greatly assisting later operations.

The D.L.I., according to orders, had moved up to the assembly trenches as the N.F. went over, with a view to supporting the attack; and I now sent a message to the commanding officer of this unit to try and work along the high ground to the left and gain ground towards the objective. About the same time I heard that there was a gap of 500 yards between us and the division who had advanced successfully. But this big gap left both divisions in the air. I therefore ordered the D.L.I. to fill the gap and secure the high ground in alignment with the captured line of the —— Division and capture the dominating enemy position on the left of our objective at Point 81. This operation was successful, a few wounded prisoners being taken.

As dusk came on I ordered the Fusiliers to push out posts in the direction of Point 81

15

and to endeavour to join up with the
D.L.I. I also ordered a platoon to be
sent to advance along the trench running
north along the western face of Contalmaison, and to endeavour to establish itself
there at the right of my intended objective
by means of a bomb attack. This platoon
came under machine gun fire, but succeeded
in occupying and consolidating a German
work on the railway, where they took a few
wounded prisoners.

The D.L.I., after dark, assaulted and took
the German redoubt at Point 81, and consolidated, sending back three wounded
prisoners. This was very encouraging, as
hitherto a machine gun at that point had
been a most powerful obstacle to our advance.

My position was now much improved, as
we held the high ground on the left of our
objective, the redoubt within the left of the
objective, and two works well forward in the
valley, and we were therefore more or less
protected by a continuous line.

Posts were pushed out along the German
trench running north to Hill 81, but consolidation was rendered very difficult owing
to a heavy rain, which turned the earth into
a sticky bog.

It was now reported that our booty in the valley included several hundred rounds of German shell, which was safely protected by one of our advanced posts already referred to.

# CHAPTER VIII

## OUR ATTACK SUCCEEDS

ON July 8th consolidation went forward. At 1.30 p.m. I was ordered to occupy Bailiff Wood. I ordered the D.L.I., who had relieved the N.F. during the night, to send out strong fighting patrols, but not to involve the whole battalion without further orders.

These patrols found the wood occupied on its southern face and came under heavy machine gun fire, both from the wood, Contalmaison, and Quadrangle Trench running along the western end of Contalmaison, and the patrols came in, having suffered some casualties.

During the night the D.L.I. did a fine piece of consolidation, joining up Triangle Trench and Point 81, so that I had a continuous line for the first time from where we joined the Division on our left, thence bending back to our front jumping-off trench.

The N.F. battalion, in support, had had a

most trying time, carrying bombs, evacuat-
ing wounded, and consolidating in the wet
under a very heavy and continuous shell fire,
and had suffered many casualties without
having any sort of a show.

I now decided to try and capture the rest
of my objective, and this I determined to
attempt from the high ground of Point 81.
I ordered the Durham battalion, at that time
resting in Becourt Wood, to make this flank
attack with two companies by a bombing
attack along the trench running east from
Point 81 to Contalmaison, the rear company
to hold and consolidate the trench and facing
north, as the attack progressed, and also to
consolidate the eastern face of Bailiff Wood.
I further ordered one battalion to endeavour
to occupy the south end of Bailiff Wood
during the afternoon with a strong patrol,
so as to assist the attack of the D.L.I. after
dusk.   This patrol went out under an officer
and actually entered Bailiff Wood, and only
withdrew owing to the fact that our own
heavies apparently had not got information
of our movements and shelled the wood so
heavily that it became untenable.

The artillery plan for the night attack
was as follows : To bombard the trench from
Point 81 eastward to Contalmaison, and at

the hour of assault to lift these guns on to
the German trenches north-west of Contalmaison, and to continue from the hour of
attack an intense enfilade fire along Quadrangle Trench from Point 74 to Point 26
until 6.15 p.m.

I watched the two companies go up to the
assembly trenches from my head-quarters
in the old British line, and they were in fine
form and full of confidence. But the best-
laid plans in war are wont to be upset;
there was some delay, owing to a false alarm
of a German attack on our left.

In the meanwhile, my wire to our artillery
group was cut, and the barrage was fired as
ordered and ceased as ordered ; the result
was, that the D.L.I. attacked at about 8 p.m.
instead of 6 p.m., and without the advantage
of artillery co-operation. The Durhams proceeded with their attack and advanced east,
capturing Bailiff Wood, where a platoon was
detached to consolidate the eastern face,
and the attack succeeded in reaching a point
within fifty yards of the north-west point
of Contalmaison Village, where it came under
a heavy machine gun fire at close range,
and a strong party was seen deploying in
front.

Thinking that the brigade on the right

might have advanced in the dark, the officer commanding the attack challenged, and heard a reply in English, " It is only us "; but recognising German uniforms, he decided to attack, and rushed forward with his leading bombers, when a machine gun at Point 25 opened fire, point blank at the attackers. The Germans now counter attacked in force over the open, and as our bomb attack was strung out, it had to give way and retired, bombing all the way back to Point 13. Here the Durhams managed to extend, and opened rapid fire on the enemy; and after detaching two strong parties north to protect their flanks, returned to the attack and drove the enemy back to the point they had originally reached when the German machine gun barred further progress.

This Point we managed to block, and the whole captured trench was consolidated with the exception of the forty yards on our extreme right which was dominated by the machine gun.

Meanwhile, the flank parties advancing north from Point 13 managed to capture four guns which had been abandoned by their teams, and proceeded to dig in in front of the guns.

This adventurous little force of about a

platoon was right over the crest looking down on Pozières village, and they were heavily counter attacked next day; but twice they drove off the attackers, who also came under our machine gun fire from the north of Bailiff Wood, and the guns were safely handed over to another brigade when the Durhams were relieved the following night.

We were now in a very much stronger position, and had won practically the whole of our objective as well as the 500 yards to our left; and when it is remembered that at the commencement of these operations the brigade was absolutely in the air on both flanks, and that our left was now secure and our right well covered from Bailiff Wood and the high ground to the west, we were naturally feeling not altogether dissatisfied.

# CHAPTER IX

## CONTALMAISON

In spite of three most gallant frontal attacks by the brigade on our right, who had twice entered the village, Contalmaison still remained German. It was therefore decided that another brigade, which was the least exhausted in the division, should attack it from the ground we had captured, advancing east in the same way as we had attacked Bailiff Wood. The advantage of this method lay in the fact that troops could reach their assembly position without being observed and they had only 700 yards to go across the open; also the enemy would not be so likely to expect an attack from this direction. All day long the Boches were trying to reinforce Contalmaison, but we kept them under our fire and inflicted considerable casualties. At one time two Red Cross motor vans came up to Contalmaison; and our fury may be imagined when we saw the Germans, instead of loading up with wounded, unloading machine guns; but we were by now used to German methods, and nothing they could do would in any way surprise us. On this day (July 10th) our artillery bombarded Contalmaison and Quadrangle Trench with great effect, so much so that the enemy were driven out of Quadrangle Trench, where they immediately came under our fire, and we disposed of at least forty Germans by our rifle and machine gun fire as they bolted.

The attack advanced in fine style from the west under a well-timed barrage and the covering fire of our brigade from its previously captured positions.

Wave after wave went steadily through our lines with only slight casualties, and after advancing across the valley in quick time they rushed Quadrangle Trench and disappeared into the village, which, after some stiff hand-to-hand fighting, was completely secured.

Thus the two brigades of the New Army had succeeded in capturing the whole of the objective allotted to the division, and the great Somme advance had taken a big step forward.

On July 11th we handed over under heavy shell fire and marched back to Albert, which was being shelled as we entered our billets.

# CHAPTER X

## POZIÈRES

My head-quarters at Albert were in a café which had, in less strenuous times, been occupied, I believe, as an officers' club; but it was in rather dangerous propinquity to the railway station, which was being much used at this time; and although we had a comfortable mess and bedrooms, we soon found that the place was " unhealthy." On July 12th three high explosive shells burst within a hundreds yards of our house, and since the walls were very thin I decided that we should move on, and gave orders for everything to be packed up and clear in one hour. A further shell in the stable yard added to our agility, and immediately afterwards our horses went clattering out of the gates, and we all took our departure.

We had only vacated this charming furnished residence for half an hour before a shell got it fair and square, and most of the interior was wrecked.

We had a more peaceful time in another house, but the enemy continued to shell Albert, and what with the constant expectation of incoming shells and the incessant din of our heavies, our rest was hardly as complete as we could wish, and even so was suddenly cut short.

On July 15th we were informed that the —— Division had lost heavily, and that as we had suffered least of our division, we were to be lent to the former, which was now in the line. It is always rather upsetting when you have been through a living hell, and are expecting to go right back to rest, suddenly to have to " bout turn " and re-enter the dust and the din; but it is particularly vexatious when you are lent away from your own folk. But there it is— *C'est la guerre!* and we marched eastward again along the Albert–Bapaume Road to the Usna–Tara line of trenches. Now numerous heavies had been brought up just in rear of this line, and the noise was most fatiguing to men who were already feeling the strain which they had endured for fifteen days.

On July 15th I went up to reconnoitre our new line, which we were ordered to take over the next day, and I looked down from

Bailiff Wood straight along what was practically a continuation of the valley which we took by Contalmaison. There, at the end of this curving valley, I saw Pozières, and was struck by the extraordinary fine defensive position it made, dominating the whole of the approach up twelve hundred yards of valley which gently rose to the village of Pozières itself. Away to my right, where a division had been attacking, the old German second trench system was on high ground on the right side of the valley, and this appeared to be the most likely approach to Pozières.

On the night of July 16th, our brigade relieved the X and Y Brigades of the —— Division, both of which had been badly cut up in previous attacks. Here the supports held the Bailiff Wood line which we had captured a few days before.

The front line which we took over from one of the relieved brigades was nothing but a few holes, and afforded very bad shelter, and the whole of our system was kept under a continual shell fire of by far the fiercest description we had yet encountered on the Somme, whilst there was no communication trench dug forward from Bailiff Wood to the new line.

During the night we set to work to dig, and the Durhams managed to dig forward as far as two small spinneys on our left, and also three considerable sections of front trench were dug, although it was impossible that night to join up.

Now I had been instructed to make a frontal attack on Pozières on the morning of the 18th up the valley, but I asked leave first to attempt to capture a continuous trench which was between my line and Pozières, because it seemed to me that, if that trench was strongly held with machine guns, there was little chance of any attack being able to carry right through and capture the large village behind with my very tired brigade. My request was acceded to, and the D.L.I. were ordered to attack this trench on the night of July 17th at 8 p.m.

The artillery plan was a heavy bombardment for some time previous, and a sudden barrage fire by divisional artillery at 8 p.m., under which the D.L.I. were to advance. Something went wrong however. By the time the whole of the attackers were launched at 8.4 p.m., an intense machine gun fire was opened on the advancing infantry.

A few men only of the Durhams succeeded in reaching the enemy trench, and these were either killed or captured, the supporting waves being absolutely stopped by the fire of machine guns, estimated to be at least ten in number. Under this fire one company on the left lost every officer.

Most of the front wave succeeded in getting within forty or fifty yards of the enemy's trench, but then cross machine gun fire and wire prevented farther progress; and after dark the survivors came back after staying about an hour in No Man's Land under heavy fire.

All the wounded were brought in that night.

In view of the main attack on the village at dawn, which was still on the cards, three battalions prepared to attack; but the German trench was full of fighting troops and machine guns and apparently unaffected by our artillery; and my own view on the spot was that if the attack went on without further preparation I should not achieve my object, and my brigade would suffer very heavily. I therefore gave this view to the higher authorities, and was greatly relieved at about midnight to receive an order that the operation was cancelled.

We now set to work to try and dig a complete fire trench and jumping-off trench;

and on the days and nights of the 18th and 19th we consolidated about 1,600 yards of new trench in front, and not only included the two little spinneys on the left in our line, but gained contact with the brigades on our right and left, where previously there were gaps of several hundred yards. We also dug forward in one place to within forty yards of the centre of the German trench, where we established and fortified a post after a short fight.

This complete new system, which we dug within 250 yards of the enemy, greatly assisted the Australians in their combined and successful attack on Pozières on a later date.

My head-quarters were in the "Sausage Valley," in a deep and very stuffy German dugout, and we were subjected to a good deal of shelling by day and gas shelling, particularly, by night.

Carrying parties had a very bad time, and any one going from Brigade Head-quarters up to the line had a particularly lively hour's march, especially in the neighbourhood of Bailiff Wood, where the enemy was throwing heavy shells with lavish hand.

On July 19th we were very glad to hear that an Australian Division was coming up to relieve us; but this day was most unpleasant, as the front system and the Sausage Valley were shelled all day long; and from 5 p.m. the enemy poured gas shells into the Sausage Valley, so that all the gas drifted down to the lowest ground where my dugout was situated, and by which a whole Australian Brigade had to come.

In Brigade Head-quarters our eyes were streaming for at least seven hours, and the gas was more unpleasant than the usual tear shells, with the result that we had to keep our helmets on the whole time, and the relieving brigade of the —— Australian Division had the very unpleasant and difficult task of marching up on relief in the dark, in their gas helmets. The relief, notwithstanding, was admirably carried out, and rarely had we known greater efficiency in any relief than that by the Anzacs on this occasion.

During these days of fighting in unorganised territory, where frequently posts are thrown out some way in front or to flanks, the relief is rarely quite complete till dawn, and on this occasion I got away from the Sausage Valley at about 3 a.m., and after many hours of a gas mask it was delightful to go back in the cool of the early morning to rest.

16

I remember as we neared Becourt Wood, where my chargers were waiting, we saw a fine-looking Anzac on his horse, silhouetted against the rising sun, when he dropped his baccy pouch by accident, and the next moment he had slipped right round his seventeen-hand horse's belly, picked his pouch off the ground, and recovered his seat —a fine effort; but really, at 3 a.m., a little exacting.

Now we are in the saddle and trotting by the field guns as they herald the new day with hideous din, and on we clatter into Albert while a shell whistles over our heads and bursts a quarter of a mile ahead. When we reached the spot two huddled shapes lie across the road never to move again. But we are very tired, and there comes a time when fatigue makes your senses dull even to death and the shells which are his messengers. So at last to bed and sleep.

# CHAPTER XI

THE brigade reached Albert at 4 a.m. on July 20th, and the same day we marched back ten miles to rejoin our division, which had been resting a week in the neighbourhood of Franvillers.

At this place we were glad to receive drafts for the brigade, and so we began to reorganise. Here we were inspected by the commander of the —— Corps, who spoke to the brigade and warmly thanked all ranks for the part they had played in the two series of operations in which they had taken such a strenuous part.

Whilst here also, the funeral took place at a village near by of Major-General Ingouville Williams, a very gallant gentleman, who never seemed happy unless he was sharing the risks of the heaviest bombardment with his men.

The ceremony was very impressive, and a

distinguished company was gathered to pay
a last tribute, whilst the pipes moaned and
sobbed their parting chant to a warrior who
did not know the meaning of fear.

Our rest was, alas, far too short—only five
days—and no one had had time to recover
before we were moving again to the sound of
the guns, and on July 26th we marched from
Franvillers right up to Contalmaison and
relieved another Infantry brigade in the old
German trenches north-east of that village.

In these trenches, which were in a very
poor state, we joined the right of the Australian Division, and the dividing line was
what was known as Munster Alley—a trench
held by the enemy which ran at right angles
from our front trench straight into the
enemy's switch line.

Now, Munster Alley was the scene of very
heavy fighting, and bomb fights had swayed
to and fro up this trench and back.  A British
division had attacked up Munster Alley,
and so had the Australians, and when we
arrived the latter were having another effort,
and after advancing about fifty yards and
having a very stiff fight, had been compelled
to fall back again to their starting point.

This was the state of affairs when I took
over the line and was also ordered to relieve

the Australians in Munster Alley.  The
bomb fight, however, was so intense that the
Australians were unable to vacate the trench
until the morning of the 26th; but we
managed to assist them, and helped to bring
up bombs, etc.

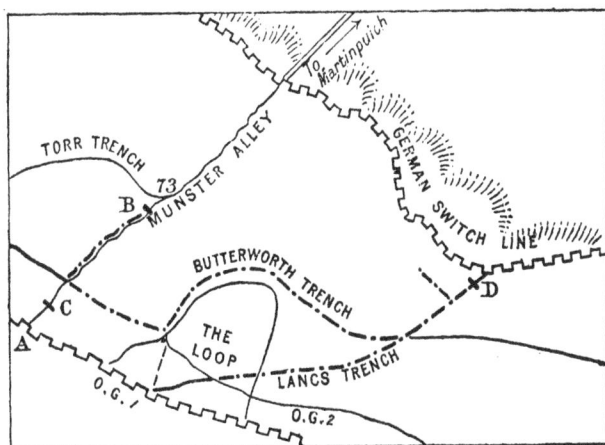

— · — · — · —  denotes final line captured and consolidated by the Brigade.
A is the point where the brigade joined the Australian 1st Division.
B is the farthest point in Munster Alley captured by the Durhams.
C is the farthest point in Munster Alley captured by the Australians.
D is the work where the N.F. commanded the slopes towards Martinpuich.
O.G.1 and O.G.2 are the old German 1st and 2nd lines which the brigade
occupied on going into this sector.

On the 27th we decided to try our hand
on Munster Alley, and the D.L.I., after a
hard bomb fight, managed to gain seventy
yards and block the trench.  We were
heavily shelled all day in the old German

system, and so we set to work at night to dig forward and deepen a ditch which went by the name of Lancs Trench, and we dug this trench, which bent forward on our right, to within fifty yards of the German switch line.

On the next night we had further fighting in Munster Alley, but without any change in the position.

We made great friends with the Australians, and one story perhaps may not be out of place to show the spirit of these lads from under the Southern Cross.

I was walking along our trench when I discovered an Australian sitting there with a bandaged hand. I asked him what he was doing. Oh, he replied, "I am resting from our bomb fight in the Alley." I then suggested that as he was wounded he had better go back to the dressing station and rest there, at which he replied that he was presently going back to the bomb fight. I told him that he was no good there with a damaged right hand, whereat he assured me he was left-handed. I then told him to remove his bandage, and found he had two fingers blown off by a bomb; so I then ordered him to go sick and shook his left hand. He was a brave man, but I fear that although I saw him " off the premises " he may have returned to the bomb fight by a circuitous route.

On the night of the 28th we were relieved, and marched back two battalions to the Sausage Valley and two to Albert, which we reached in the early hours of the morning.

## CHAPTER XII

On July 31st, we had a very jolly musical evening in a delightful house in Albert. A padre was there, and proved himself no mean performer on the piano, and one of the Durhams, who has charmed many a great audience at home before the war called him, delighted us with song. The two most cheery members of the mess were Captain Hurd-Wood, the Staff captain, who had been with the brigade since its birth, and the interpreter Lieut. de Mandiarges, a handsome, cultured Frenchman, who was very dear to us all.

To-night we are all happy like boys in an English barrack mess; to-morrow, half an hour after the brigade had left again for the line, a heavy shell, guided by the hand of fate, entered their room; the Staff captain is killed, de Mandiarges is carried off mortally wounded, to live only long enough to receive

the Croix de Guerre, whilst two other officers,
Major Botham of the Fusiliers and a young
subaltern recently out from England who
had been left behind to rest, were in that
fatal house, and they too died in that moment
for their country.

. . . . .

This time the brigade was divided, two
battalions being lent to another brigade.
The N.F. and the D.L.I. went into the line
on our front and two battalions of another
brigade were lent me as reserves.

During the night of August 4th a company
of the N.F. on the extreme right pushed a
post forward to within a few yards of the
switch line, and from here, looking down
on Martinpuich, dominated the German
approach to the switch line. During this
day and the next they inflicted with
picked marksmen considerable losses on the
enemy, which losses were estimated at well
over a hundred, whilst our machine guns
accounted for another thirty. Here an unusual incident took place, the Germans
coming out with a big Red Cross flag, and
we allowed them all day to gather and carry
in their wounded.

I was very glad to have this opportunity
of returning to civilised warfare; but how

hopeless was this desire will be related later, for next morning the Germans once more reciprocated by adopting tactics to which no savage warrior of the past would ever descend.

All that day our heavies bombarded the enemy switch line in front of us and the Australians.

I decided to attack Munster Alley simultaneously with a bombing attack from our junction with the Anzacs, going north-east, and another attack over the top from our new jumping-off trenches by the loop in Butterworth Trench, attacking north-west. Some three hours before the attack I relieved the N.F., holding the jumping-off trenches, by the D.L.I.; but unfortunately, after the relief was complete, these trenches were very heavily shelled, being almost entirely obliterated in parts; and as this shelling went on until the hour for attack, the attacking company was badly shaken when the hour arrived.

The attack commenced, and the company advanced from the loop trench and nearly reached their objective under our barrage, when a heavy fire was opened from a German trench, which, not having been bombarded, was full of Germans. To add to the

confusion all the smoke and dust of the
Australian bombardment drifted back on
the Durhams, who could not see their officers
and found themselves under a heavy machine
gun and bomb fire. Captain Austen, the
gallant company commander, pressed on
with the few men round him and reached
the German trench, and was never seen
again, whilst the subaltern on his flank
was hit, and the front wave wavered and
began to retire.

The supporting platoons, advancing into
the dust and under heavy fire, seeing the
front waves retiring, and not knowing the
commander was killed, thought a retirement
was ordered, and returned to their trenches,
when, if there had been an officer on the spot
to control the situation, they must have
gained their objective.

Meanwhile the bomb attack of the other
company forged ahead and gained seventy
yards, killing numerous Germans and suc-
ceeding in blocking the trench where they had
gained ground nearly up to the point of their
objective, after an exceedingly bloody and
brilliant attack. Simultaneously the Australians had swept on and taken the windmill, and even penetrated beyond.

We tried to organise another attack that

night to gain the rest of the objective, but our trenches were so damaged by the shelling above referred to, and so blocked by casualties, that I had to abandon the attempt.

Before light I went up to the line to find out the exact situation, and I reached it at dawn, proceeding to Munster Alley, where the Durhams had advanced. Here I discovered that the Germans were perpetrating their most dastardly crime, bombing our wounded where they lay around the trench we had assaulted the previous evening. When it is remembered that all the previous day we had allowed them to carry in their wounded, the rage of our men can be imagined, and I am glad to say they succeeded in shooting several enemy bombers who exposed themselves in their wicked work.

Captain Clarke of the Durhams, who had previously won the Military Cross and who had been fighting all night, showed me the ground where the attack had taken place, and then I went up to the farthest point reached with Lieut. Kaye-Butterworth, also of the Durhams. The trench was very low and broken, and he kept on urging me to keep low down. I had only reached the Battalion Head-quarters on my return when

I heard poor Butterworth, a brilliant musician in times of peace, and an equally brilliant soldier in times of stress, was shot dead by a bullet through the head. So he who had been so thoughtful for my safety had suffered the fate he had warned me against only a minute before.

It was now getting quite light, and as I looked towards the distant windmill, now only a mass of stones, I saw a considerable number of men coming over the rise from towards Martinpuich. I thought it must be a counter-attack, and turned to a gunner by my side, who lent me his glasses. There, sure enough, were the grey uniforms of Germans; but now most of the figures halted, lay down and faced the enemy, apparently firing, and then I realised by their slouch hats that this was the return of an Australian "hunting expedition," and that they were bringing back several German prisoners, whom they must have extracted from positions far past their objective.

A little later in the day, the Germans made a small counter-attack against the new Durham position. Now this was precisely what the Durhams wanted, as they were anxious to kill Germans; but although it was no affair of theirs, numerous Australians jumped out of their trenches and proceeded to charge towards the Germans, who by that time were easily repulsed by our fire.

There is no doubt that the Anzac is keen, for this was after all-night fighting !

That night we were relieved, and now at last, after thirty-five days' fighting or being shelled, during which time we had only had five days' rest behind our guns, we marched, on August 8th, away from these bloody scenes and stayed at amazingly peaceful villages in the rear—in another world, where the eternal drab is replaced by the green of an innocent countryside.

# CHAPTER XIII

## CONCLUSION

I CANNOT leave my disjointed attempt to give my impressions of my sojourn amongst our fighters without some small but very inadequate tribute to the spirit of our great Army.

For sixteen months as a regimental officer and six as a brigade commander, I have lived amongst officers, non-commissioned officers, and men in the strange life which is limited for such long periods by earth walls. I have received, given, and seen carried out the orders to advance; I have known the crowded incidents of digging, for dear life, a newly captured line within two hundred yards of the Germans; I have waited for the dawn which will deluge you in a rain of tons of terrible metal accompanied by its tornado of sound; I have crouched for long hours whilst the mad dance of death swirls round you, front and behind, to right and left,

when you pray for the night. Hundreds of
hours I have spent in the trenches, seeing
and wondering at that great-hearted gentleman the British soldier, and so I may claim
to speak from knowledge of what things are
there at the heart of things.

Never have I seen a single incident of a
fit man in the great Army which has lessened
my faith in my countrymen or caused me to
feel shame for the flag of our race.

I have seen men, it is true, with nerves
shattered and trembling like children, unable
to go on facing the fight, but in those cases
I know that they have been put to a greater
test than mortal man is meant to bear, and
that the man who is seriously concussed
by shell-shock is as truly out of action
as the man who has a bullet through his
chest.

The fortitude of our wounded is the
wonder of all who have seen, and it is only
beaten by the manner of those who lie down
to die.

The selfishness of the old world is left far
behind, and soldier shares with soldier all
the small things which make life bearable,
and often a tired man will offer to carry
the rifle or kit of a comrade to prevent him
falling out on the march.

I remember a division which had been fighting with heavy losses being ordered up again unexpectedly on the Somme, and the day they went into action the average sickness fell from two or three hundred to one man sick. What finer evidence could we require to prove the honour of those 20,000 men ?

Who has watched a battalion march to the line and has not noticed the delightful humour which runs through all ranks, and who has seen the line of bayonets ready to jump the parapet and has not realised how much of the God there is in every man ?

What company commander is there who has had to ask in vain for volunteers to go out in the night and gather in wounded from No Man's Land ? Indeed, what commander is there who has not had difficulty in cutting down the number of volunteers when the lives of comrades are at stake ?

War may be a hateful thing, but only the luckless who are strangers to its meaning can deny its ennobling influence, provided the cause is righteous, or that, in spite of all the devastating horrors, all the sorrows and tears, the world will be enriched by the return of the survivors of our wonderful Army.

17

Yes, comrades of mine, you have marched down a long, long road, but you have this consolation, that you have never faltered. You may swear and grumble at times, but that does not belittle the fact that in the greatest cause for which man ever gave himself, you have with a song and a joke faced such things as man never previously dreamed of.

Hundreds, thousands, scores of thousands, of our mates have left you to go far West, and at times we feel almost overwhelmed with grief; but should we mourn too much for them, for, whatever their lives may have been, have they not absolutely made good, and is not the way of their going—those young, brave lads—such that they have succeeded in solving the greatest mystery which faces the frail creatures of this earth : have they not renewed the hope of mankind in giving their lives for their friends ?

For you who return, there is a great trust, for as you have saved, so shall you build ; you at least have no " Craven fear of being great " ; and, with those fine brothers of ours who have come from the far places of the earth to stand by your side in the line, you will set out to make these Islands and the outer Empire a greater, happier place, and so the faith which called you in the hour of decision will give you power to enrich the world by consummating the union of the battlefield and the grave in the lasting union of the British brotherhood.

PRINTED BY
HAZELL, WATSON AND VINEY, LD.,
LONDON AND AYLESBURY,
ENGLAND.

*9 781847 341679*